The Shurangama Sutra

Volume Six

The Shurangama Sutra

Volume Six

with commentary by the
Venerable Master Hsuan Hua

A nine book series

First Edition, 2003
Sutra Text and Supplements, Volumes 1 to 8

English translation by the
Buddhist Text Translation Society
ISBN 0-88139-949-3

The Shurangama Sutra - Volume Six

Published and translated by:

Buddhist Text Translation Society
1777 Murchison Drive, Burlingame, CA 94010-4504

© 2003 **Buddhist Text Translation Society
Dharma Realm Buddhist University
Dharma Realm Buddhist Association**

First edition 2003

12 11 10 09 08 07 06 05 04 03   10 9 8 7 6 5 4 3 2 1

ISBN 0-88139-946-9

Printed in Malaysia.

Addresses of the Dharma Realm Buddhist Association branches are listed at the back of this book.

Library of Congress Cataloging-in-Publication Data

Hsüan Hua, 1908-
 The Shurangama sutra with commentary / by Hsuan Hua ; English translation by the Buddhist Text Translation Society.-- 1st ed.
  p. cm.
 Sutra translated from Chinese, originally written in Sanskrit. "The Shurangama sutra/ Sutra & suppliments" (ISBN 0-88139-940-X) issued together.
  ISBN 0-88139-949-3 (set : alk. paper) -- ISBN 0-88139-941-8 (v. 1 : alk. paper) -- ISBN 0-88139-942-6 (v. 2 : alk. paper) -- ISBN 0-88139-943-4 (v. 3 : alk. paper) -- ISBN 0-88139-944-2 (v. 4 : alk. paper) -- ISBN 0-88139-945-0 (v. 5 : alk. paper) -- ISBN 0-88139-946-9 (v. 6 : alk. paper) -- ISBN 0-88139-947-7 (v. 7 : alk. paper) -- ISBN 0-88139-948-5 (v. 8 : alk. paper)
 1. Tripiṭaka. Sūtrapiṭaka. Sūraṅgamasūtra--Commentaries. I. Buddhist Text Translation Society. II. Tripiṭaka. Sūtrapiṭaka. Sūraṅgamasūtra. English. III. Title.

BQ2127.H7813 2003
294.3'85--dc21

2002151845

Contents

Introduction vi
User's Guide viii
Exhortation to Protect and Propagate ix
The Eight Guidelines xii
Outline xiii

Chapter 1. The Three Non-Outflow Studies 1
    One Must Cut Off Lust 10
    One Must Cut Off Killing 19
    One Must Cut Off Stealing 30
    One Must Cut Off False Speech 47

Chapter 2. Establishing the Bodhimanda 73

Chapter 3. The Spiritual Mantra 85

Chapter 4. The Two Upside-down Causes 159

Chapter 5. The Twelve Categories of Living Beings 174

General Index 191

Introduction

This is Volume Six of the *Shurangama Sutra* series, with commentaries by the Venerable Master Hsuan Hua.

Ananda, having gained what he had never before, wishes to propagate the teachings and save living beings. However, he is concerned that demonic teachers of the present and future will also propound their deviant theories, thus misleading and exploiting living beings. Ananda asks how does one protect oneself from such teachings.

In "The Three Non-Outflow Studies," the Buddha explains how disciplining the mind via precepts, which in turn produces samadhi, which in turn produces wisdom are the three unalterable aspects of cultivation. Of the precepts, he stresses that one must specifically cut off lust, killing, stealing and false speech. Anything not in accord with this is the teaching of the demons.

Ananda then asks how living beings in the Dharma-ending Age can establish a Way place (*bodhimanda*) so that living beings can safely cultivate in accord with the Buddha's rules of purity. In "Establishing the Bodhimanda," the Buddha explains just how to do that.

Ananda then, remembering how Manjushri saved him from the then-prostitute daughter of Matangi by using a spiritual mantra, requests that the Buddha declares it for the benefit and protection of future living beings. In "The Spiritual Mantra," the mantra is preciously proclaimed. After its proclamation, bodhisattvas, gods, kings, and other great spiritual beings resolve to protect all those of the present and future who uphold the spiritual mantra.

Now that Ananda has secured the means to protect people's cultivation from the multitudes of demons (through the use of the non-outflow studies, the bodhimanda and the spiritual mantra), he then proceeds to ask the Buddha how one can ascertain one's own progress from an ordinary person to final nirvana.

In response, the Buddha does not immediately speak of the stages of cultivation.[i] Instead, the Buddha first explains about the "The Two Upside-down Causes." If the cultivator does not produce these two states, then one is cultivating in proper samadhi, regardless of stage. If one does produce these two states, then even if one ascends through the stages of cultivation, it will be improper.

The two causes are: the upside-down state of living beings and the upside-down state of the world. In "The Twelve Categories of Living Beings," the Buddha explains how these two upside-down states produce the twelve categories of living beings that abound throughout the world.

[i.] The stages of cultivation are covered in volume seven.

User's Guide

to the Shurangama Sutra series

Because of the length of the *Shurangama Sutra*, and the need to provide aid to various readers, the sutra has been compiled into a series of 9 books: the "Sutra Text and Supplements," and the remaining volumes one to eight.

The "Sutra Text and Supplements" contains:

1. the entire sutra text, consisting of over 2700 paragraphs;
2. the entire outline, consisting of over 1670 entries; and
3. a master index for the eight commentarial volumes.

Volumes one to eight contain:

1. sutra text, with commentaries by Venerable Master Hua;
2. local outline entries; and
3. a local index.

Readers who wish to read, study or recite the sutra in its entirety will find the "Sutra Text and Supplements" very useful.

Those who wish to deeply delve into the sutra will find the commentaries in volumes one to eight indispensable.

Exhortation to Protect and Propagate

by Tripitaka Master Hsuan Hua

Within Buddhism, there are very many important sutras. However, the most important sutra is the *Shurangama Sutra*. If there are places which have the *Shurangama Sutra*, then the proper dharma dwells in the world. If there is no *Shurangama Sutra*, then the dharma ending age appears. Therefore, we Buddhist disciples, each and every one, must bring our strength, must bring our blood, and must bring our sweat to protect the *Shurangama Sutra*. In the *Sutra of the Ultimate Extinction of the Dharma*, it says very, very clearly that in the dharma ending age, the *Shurangama Sutra* is the first to disappear, and the rest of the sutras disappear after it. If the *Shurangama Sutra* does not disappear, then the proper dharma age is present. Because of that, we Buddhist disciples must use our lives to protect the *Shurangama Sutra*. We must use vows and resolution to protect the *Shurangama Sutra*, and cause the *Shurangama Sutra* to be known far and wide, reaching every nook and cranny, reaching into each and every dust-mote, reaching out to the exhaustion of empty space and of the dharma realm. If we can do that, then there will be a time of proper dharma radiating great light.

Why would the *Shurangama Sutra* be destroyed? It is because it is too true. The *Shurangama Sutra* is the Buddha's true body. The *Shurangama Sutra* is the Buddha's sharira. The *Shurangama Sutra* is the Buddha's true and actual stupa and shrine. Therefore, because the *Shurangama Sutra* is so true, all the demon kings use all kinds of methods to destroy the *Shurangama Sutra*. They begin by starting rumors, saying that the *Shurangama Sutra* is phony. Why do they say the *Shurangama Sutra* is phony? It is because the *Shurangama Sutra* speaks too truly, especially in the sections on the Four Decisive Deeds, the Twenty-five Sages Describing Perfect Penetration, and the States of the Fifty Skandha Demons. Those of off-center persuasions and externally-oriented ways, weird demons and strange freaks, are unable to stand it. Consequently, there are a good many senseless people who claim that the *Shurangama Sutra* is a forgery.

Now, the principles set forth in the *Shurangama Sutra* are on the one hand proper, and on the other in accord with principle, and the weird demons and strange freaks, those in various cults and sects, all cannot hide away their forms. Most senseless people, in particular the unwise scholars and garbage-collecting professors, "tread upon the holy writ." With their extremely scant and partial understanding, they are confused and unclear, lacking real erudition and true and actual wisdom. That is why they falsely criticize. We who study the Buddhadharma should very deeply be aware of these circumstances. Therefore, wherever we go, we should bring up the *Shurangama Sutra*. Wherever we go, we should propagate the *Shurangama Sutra*. Wherever we go, we should introduce the *Shurangama Sutra* to people. Why is that? It is because we wish to cause the proper dharma to dwell long in the world.

If the *Shurangama Sutra* is regarded as true, then there is no problem. To verify its truth, let me say that if the *Shurangama Sutra* were phony, then I would willingly fall into the hells forever through all eternity – for being unable to recognize the Buddhadharma – for mistaking the false for true. If the *Shurangama Sutra* is true, then life after life in every time I make the vow to propagate the great dharma of the Shurangama, that I shall in every time and every place propagate the true principles of the Shurangama.

Everyone should pay attention to the following point. How could the *Shurangama Sutra* not have been spoken by the Buddha?

No one else could have spoken the *Shurangama Sutra*. And so I hope that all those people who make senseless accusations will wake up fast and stop creating the causes for suffering in the Hell of Pulling Out Tongues. No matter who the scholar is, no matter what country students of the Buddhadharma are from, all should quickly mend their ways, admit their mistakes, and manage to change. There is no greater good than that. I can then say that all who look at the *Shurangama Sutra*, all who listen to the *Shurangama Sutra*, and all who investigate the *Shurangama Sutra*, will very quickly accomplish Buddhahood.

composed by,
Gold Mountain Shramana Tripitaka Master Hua

The Eight Guidelines

of the Buddhist Text Translation Society

1. A volunteer must free him/herself from the motives of personal fame and profit.
2. A volunteer must cultivate a respectful and sincere attitude free from arrogance and conceit.
3. A volunteer must refrain from aggrandizing his/her work and denigrating that of others.
4. A volunteer must not establish him/herself as the standard of correctness and suppress the work of others with his or her fault-finding.
5. A volunteer must take the Buddha-mind as his/her own mind.
6. A volunteer must use the wisdom of Dharma-selecting Vision to determine true principles.
7. A volunteer must request Virtuous Elders in the ten directions to certify his/her translations.
8. A volunteer must endeavour to propagate the teachings by printing Sutras, Shastra texts, and Vinaya texts when the translations are certified as being correct.

Outline

of the Shurangama Sutra

The outline for the *Shurangama Sutra*, compiled by Dharma Master Yuan Ying, categorizes the various parts of the sutra text of over 2,700 paragraphs to over 1,670 entries.

These entries are presented in the form of a tree-like structure which divides the various parts of the sutra text into sections and sub-sections.

Though the outline is not a prerequisite to reading the sutra text and the accompanying commentaries, it serves as a useful tool for students of the Way who wish to systematically study the sutra. Without this outline, students may find it difficult to refer to specific parts of the text.

Only outline entries which pertain to the sutra text contained within this volume is included.

For the outline of the entire sutra, please refer to the "Sutra Text and Supplements."

Outline of Shurangama Sutra – Volume Six

```
G2 Aiding practices of the bodhimanda. .......................................................... 1
  H1 At first request he speaks in general. ...................................................... 1
  H2 On second request he speaks in detail. ................................................... 3
    I1 Ananda asks. ........................................................................................ 3
    I2 The Thus Come One answers. .............................................................. 5
      J1 He promises to speak; they wish to listen. ......................................... 5
      J2 He brings up the three studies in general. .......................................... 7
      J3 He specifically lists the three studies. ............................................... 10
        K1 He lists the importance of the precepts first. ................................. 10
          L1 He teaches him to hold precepts. ................................................ 10
            M1 He gathers in first and then gives evidence. ............................. 10
              N1 One must cut off lust. ............................................................. 10
                O1 Distinguishes the characteristic harm and benefit. ............... 10
                  P1 First he explains the benefit or harm of holding or violating. ... 10
                    Q1 Holding it, then one certainly can get out of birth and death. .. 10
                    Q2 Violating it, one certainly will fall into demonic paths. ........... 11
                  P2 He discusses the behavior of demons within Buddhism. ........ 13
                    Q1 Greed for lust turns the world. ............................................... 13
                    Q2 Teaching people to cut off lust is the Buddha's instruction. ..... 14
                  P3 Decides if the bodhimanda can be accomplished. .................... 15
                    Q1 An analogy shows that if one doesn't cut off lust, bodhi can't be obtained. .. 15
                    Q2 Diligently and profoundly cutting off lust can bring accomplishment. .. 18
                O2 He speaks of the divisions of deviant and proper. .................... 18
              N2 One must cut off killing. ............................................................. 19
                O1 He distinguishes the characteristic harm and benefit. ............. 19
                  P1 First he explains the benefit or harm of holding or violating. .. 19
                    Q1 Holding it, then one certainly can get out of birth and death. .. 19
                    Q2 Violating it, one certainly will fall into demons within Buddhism. .. 19
                  P2 He discusses the behavior of demons within Buddhism. ........ 21
                    Q1 Eating flesh turns the world into a teaching by ghosts. .......... 21
```

```
            Q2  Teaching people to cut off killing is the Buddha's instruction. . . . . . . . . . . . . . . . . . . 24
         P3 He decides if liberation can be obtained. . . . . . . . . . . . . . . . . . . . . . . . . . . . . . . . . . . . . . 25
            Q1  An analogy makes clear, if one doesn't cut off killing it is difficult to get free. . . . . . . 25
            Q2  If one diligently and profoundly cuts off killing, one can get free. . . . . . . . . . . . . . . 26
      O2 He speaks of the division into deviant and proper. . . . . . . . . . . . . . . . . . . . . . . . . . . . . . . . . 28
   N3 One must cut off stealing. . . . . . . . . . . . . . . . . . . . . . . . . . . . . . . . . . . . . . . . . . . . . . . . . . . . . . . . . . 30
      O1 He distinguishes the characteristic harm and benefit. . . . . . . . . . . . . . . . . . . . . . . . . . . . . . . 30
         P1 First he discusses the benefit or harm of holding or violating. . . . . . . . . . . . . . . . . . . . . . 30
            Q1  Holding it, one then certainly can get out of birth and death. . . . . . . . . . . . . . . . . . 30
            Q2  Violating it, one certainly will fall into deviant paths. . . . . . . . . . . . . . . . . . . . . . . . . 31
         P2 He discusses the behavior of weird beings within Buddhism. . . . . . . . . . . . . . . . . . . . . . . 34
            Q1  Hidden influences are the teachings of weird beings. . . . . . . . . . . . . . . . . . . . . . . . . 34
            Q2  Teaching people to cut off stealing is the Buddha's instruction. . . . . . . . . . . . . . . . 41
               R1  First he offers his own instructions. . . . . . . . . . . . . . . . . . . . . . . . . . . . . . . . . . . . . . 41
               R2  Then he explains it is the teaching of all former Buddhas. . . . . . . . . . . . . . . . . . . 43
         P3 He decides if samadhi can be obtained. . . . . . . . . . . . . . . . . . . . . . . . . . . . . . . . . . . . . . . . 44
            Q1  An analogy makes clear that if stealing is not cut off, samadhi is hard to obtain. . 44
            Q2  Diligent and profound cutting off of stealing can bring samadhi. . . . . . . . . . . . . . . 44
   N4 One must cut off false speech. . . . . . . . . . . . . . . . . . . . . . . . . . . . . . . . . . . . . . . . . . . . . . . . . . . . . 47
      O1 He discusses the intent of precepts or provisional teachings. . . . . . . . . . . . . . . . . . . . . . . . . 47
         P1 False speech is very harmful. . . . . . . . . . . . . . . . . . . . . . . . . . . . . . . . . . . . . . . . . . . . . . . . . 47
            Q1  Traces false speech as a reason for becoming demonic. . . . . . . . . . . . . . . . . . . . . . . 47
            Q2  Points out the motives of false speech. . . . . . . . . . . . . . . . . . . . . . . . . . . . . . . . . . . . 48
            Q3  Predicts the fall of those who harm the good. . . . . . . . . . . . . . . . . . . . . . . . . . . . . . 50
         P2 He shows that he has clearly instructed against false speech. . . . . . . . . . . . . . . . . . . . . . 51
            Q1  The Buddha instructs that holy transformations must be secret. . . . . . . . . . . . . . . . 51
            Q2  Only at the end of their life is there a transmission. . . . . . . . . . . . . . . . . . . . . . . . . 58
         P3 The clear instruction transmitted from former Buddhas. . . . . . . . . . . . . . . . . . . . . . . . . . . 60
         P4 Deciding if bodhi can be obtained. . . . . . . . . . . . . . . . . . . . . . . . . . . . . . . . . . . . . . . . . . . . 60
            Q1  An analogy shows that if one does not cut off false speech, it is difficult to obtain bodhi. . 60
```

Outline of Shurangama Sutra – Volume Six

```
       Q2 He promises if one can cut off false speech, one will certainly accomplish bodhi. . . . . . . . 63
          O2 He speaks of the division into deviant and proper. . . . . . . . . . . . . . . . . . . . . . . . . . . . . . . 64
             M3 General conclusion: stay distant from demons. . . . . . . . . . . . . . . . . . . . . . . . . . . . . . 64
             L2 Aided by the power of the mantra. . . . . . . . . . . . . . . . . . . . . . . . . . . . . . . . . . . . . . . . 65
                M1 Supreme praise for diligently holding it. . . . . . . . . . . . . . . . . . . . . . . . . . . . . . . . . 65
                M2 He also shows it is not difficult to get rid of these habits. . . . . . . . . . . . . . . . . . . 68
             K2 A general explanation of samadhi and wisdom in the bodhimanda. . . . . . . . . . . . . 69
                L1 Because of precepts one produces samadhi. . . . . . . . . . . . . . . . . . . . . . . . . . . . 69
                L2 Because of samadhi one opens wisdom. . . . . . . . . . . . . . . . . . . . . . . . . . . . . . . . 71
          G2 At second request he explains in detail. . . . . . . . . . . . . . . . . . . . . . . . . . . . . . . . . . . . . . 73
             H1 At second request he describes the bodhimanda. . . . . . . . . . . . . . . . . . . . . . . . . . . . 73
                I1 Ananda asks again. . . . . . . . . . . . . . . . . . . . . . . . . . . . . . . . . . . . . . . . . . . . . . . . . . 73
                I2 The World Honored One answers again. . . . . . . . . . . . . . . . . . . . . . . . . . . . . . . . . 74
                   J1 Establishing the bodhimanda. . . . . . . . . . . . . . . . . . . . . . . . . . . . . . . . . . . . . . . 74
                      K1 The platform. . . . . . . . . . . . . . . . . . . . . . . . . . . . . . . . . . . . . . . . . . . . . . . . . 74
                      K2 The adornments. . . . . . . . . . . . . . . . . . . . . . . . . . . . . . . . . . . . . . . . . . . . . . 75
                      K3 The offerings. . . . . . . . . . . . . . . . . . . . . . . . . . . . . . . . . . . . . . . . . . . . . . . . 76
                      K4 The mirrors. . . . . . . . . . . . . . . . . . . . . . . . . . . . . . . . . . . . . . . . . . . . . . . . . . 80
                   J2 Stages of cultivation and accomplishment. . . . . . . . . . . . . . . . . . . . . . . . . . . . . 80
                      K1 First three weeks: initial accomplishment of samadhi and wisdom. . . . . . . . 80
                      K2 After one hundred more days: sudden certification to the sagely fruit. . . . . 82
                      K3 Concludes answer to question. . . . . . . . . . . . . . . . . . . . . . . . . . . . . . . . . . . . 84
             H2 On second request he speaks the spiritual mantra. . . . . . . . . . . . . . . . . . . . . . . . . . . 85
                I1 The entire assembly asks again. . . . . . . . . . . . . . . . . . . . . . . . . . . . . . . . . . . . . . . 85
                I2 The Thus Come One answers again. . . . . . . . . . . . . . . . . . . . . . . . . . . . . . . . . . . . 89
                   J1 He speaks the spiritual mantra. . . . . . . . . . . . . . . . . . . . . . . . . . . . . . . . . . . . . . 89
                      K1 An appearance of light. . . . . . . . . . . . . . . . . . . . . . . . . . . . . . . . . . . . . . . . . 89
                      K2 The great assembly respectfully listens. . . . . . . . . . . . . . . . . . . . . . . . . . . . . 91
                      K3 The five sections of the spiritual mantra. . . . . . . . . . . . . . . . . . . . . . . . . . . . 94
                   J2 He speaks of the benefits of the mantra. . . . . . . . . . . . . . . . . . . . . . . . . . . . . . . 113
```

K1 The important tool of all Buddhas. 113
   L1 He explains the entire name. 113
   L2 He states its functions. 114
   L3 Further explanations are endless. 120
K2 A beneficial reliance for living beings. 120
   L1 Specific explanation of the supreme name. 120
   L2 A thorough discussion of its awesome power. 121
      M1 He first explains that by diligently holding it, cultivators can rely on it. ...121
         N1 He explains that recitation of it will keep demons away. 121
         N2 Writing it out and carrying it is of benefit. 121
      M2 A detailed account of the ways in which it protects life and aids people on the path. ...122
         N1 General mention of these two aspects. 122
         N2 Detailed listing of its many merits. 123
            O1 Apparent benefit to each living being. 123
               P1 Rescues from calamities. 123
                   Q1 Evil situations cannot bring harm. 123
                   Q2 Evil beings cannot break through its added protection to cause harm. ...123
               P2 Aids in accomplishing way karma. 127
                   Q1 The value of its recitation. 127
                   Q2 Separation from various destinies. 129
                   Q3 Always born where there are Buddhas. 131
                   Q4 Various practices are accomplished. 133
                   Q5 All offenses are eradicated. 135
                   Q6 Quick certification to non-production. 140
               P3 Answers all kinds of wishes. 141
            O2 Apparent universal benefit to the land. 144
               P1 All difficulties disappear. 144
               P2 The people experience plenty and happiness. 146
               P3 Evil omens do not manifest. 146
      M3 He makes clear with a general exhortation that cultivators will certainly certify. ...150

Outline of Shurangama Sutra – Volume Six

Outline of Shurangama Sutra – Volume Six

```
            N1  They will be protected and peaceful..........................................150
            N2  They will be far apart from demons and enemies...................150
            N3  They will not commit four violations.......................................151
            N4  They must keep their minds on their recitation......................151
      I3  The assembly vows to protect it.......................................................152
         J1  The outer assembly protects and holds it.....................................152
            K1  The multitude of vajra power-knights.....................................152
            K2  The venerable hosts of gods....................................................152
            K3  The host of the eight divisions................................................153
            K4  The ruling assembly of illumining bodies...............................153
            K5  The deities and spirits of the earth..........................................154
         J2  The inner sages protect and hold it................................................155
            K1  They reveal their origin and their long-term protection........155
            K2  They assert their protection and maintaining.........................155
               F4  He explains certification to the position of dhyana causing him to dwell
                     in complete samadhi and tend straight toward bodhi.................159
   G1  Ananda is grateful for the instruction and asks about the position..........159
   G2  The Thus Come One answers with instruction in the arisal of conditions......161
      H1  The Thus Come One offers to speak and the great assembly waits to hear....161
      H2  The true suchness which is relied upon is the source of the dharma..........163
      H3  Defiled conditions arise and become the turning wheel......................164
         I1  He exhorts Ananda to recognize two causes for being upside-down.......164
         I2  He clarified the two causes for being upside-down, in detail..............165
            J1  He makes it clear that living beings are upside-down..................165
               K1  From the true true they give rise to the false........................165
               K2  They confuse their origin so it is difficult to return..............167
               K3  They produce karma which brings a retribution..................169
            J2  He makes clear the world is upside-down................................170
               K1  He explains the meaning of the word world.......................170
               K2  He shows its characteristic is constant flux.........................171
```

K3 He explains the retributions of the categories of beings.	174
L1 He lists the names of the categories of beings.	174
L2 He explains the retributions of the categories of beings.	176
M1 A specific listing of the categories of beings.	176
N1 Egg-born.	176
N2 Womb-born.	177
N3 Moisture-born.	178
N4 Transformation-born.	179
N5 Having form.	180
N6 Without form.	181
N7 Having thought.	182
N8 Without thought.	183
N9 Not totally having form.	184
N10 Not totally without form.	185
N11 Not totally with thought.	186
N12 Not totally without thought.	187
M2 Reiterates their name and number.	188

釋迦牟尼文佛

Namo Original Teacher Shakyamuni Buddha

Verse for Opening a Sutra

*The unsurpassed, profound, and wonderful dharma,
Is difficult to encounter in hundreds of millions of eons,
I now see and hear it, receive and uphold it,
And I vow to fathom the Tathagata's true meaning.*

CHAPTER 1

The Three Non-Outflow Studies

G2 Aiding practices of the bodhimanda.
H1 At first request he speaks in general.

Sutra:

    Ananda straightened his robes and then bowed in the midst of the assembly and placed his palms together. The tracks of his mind were perfectly clear, and he felt a mixture of joy and sorrow. His intent was to benefit beings in the future as he made obeisance and said to the Buddha, "Greatly compassionate World Honored One, I have already awakened and received this teaching for becoming a Buddha, and I can cultivate it without the slightest doubt. I have often heard the Thus Come One say, 'Save others first then save yourself. That is the aspiration of a bodhisattva. Once your own enlightenment is perfected, then you can enlighten others. That is the way the Thus Come One responds to the world.' Although I am not yet saved, I vow to save all living beings in the Dharma-ending Age.

Commentary:

    After **Ananda** had listened to Manjushri Bodhisattva's verse, he stood up and **straightened his robes**. He fixed his collar and arranged his robes. He was never sloppy or careless, never let his clothes get messed up. **And then** he **bowed in the midst of the**

assembly and placed his palms together. The tracks of his mind were perfectly clear. Ananda was not as confused as he was previously, **and he felt a mixture of joy and sorrow. His intent was to benefit beings in the future as he made obeisance and said to the Buddha.** Ananda didn't know whether to laugh or cry. Do you remember how easily Ananda cries? He has already cried several times since the start of the sutra, and now he wants to cry again. But he also feels like laughing. What was his sorrow? As it is said:

> Joy in extreme gives rise to sorrow.

He was totally happy, thinking, "Now I have the Buddhadharma! I understand the genuine dharma!" He had never felt such joy. But it wasn't enough to understand for himself; he wanted to benefit beings of the future. So he made obeisance to the Buddha and said: **Greatly compassionate World Honored One, I have already awakened and received this teaching for becoming a Buddha, and I can cultivate it without the slightest doubt.** I will cultivate by means of the dharma and will never have any more doubts.

I have often heard the Thus Come One say. Ananda always has to substantiate what he says by making reference to the Buddha's own teaching. He says here, "I've heard the Buddha say, **'Save others first, then save yourself. That is the aspiration of a bodhisattva.'"** Before one has attained the Way, one can go ahead and teach others. That's the way a bodhisattva does it. **Once your own enlightenment is perfected, then you can enlighten others. That is the way the Thus Come One responds to the world.** You help others wake up by means of the principles that you have awakened to. This is what the Buddha does. **Although I am not yet saved, I vow to save all living beings in the Dharma-ending Age.** I haven't attained the Way yet, but I want to enable all beings in the final age to be taken across. I want them to attain the benefits of the Buddhadharma.

H2　On second request he speaks in detail.
I1　Ananda asks.

Sutra:

"World Honored One, those living beings will gradually drift away from the Buddha, and there will be as many deviant teachers propounding their methods as there are sands in the Ganges. I want to enable those beings to collect their thoughts and enter samadhi. How can I cause them to reside peacefully in a bodhimanda, far from the exploits of demons, and be irreversible in their resolve for bodhi?"

Commentary:

World Honored One, those living beings will gradually drift away from the Buddha. Beings in the Dharma-ending Age will gradually end up being very far away from the Buddha and even the Buddhadharma. **There will be as many deviant teachers propounding their methods as there are sands in the Ganges.** That's the way it is now. Deviant teachers claim to understand things that they actually do not understand. Not enlightened, they say that they are. Not certified as sages, they say that they are. I ask them, "Have you been certified to the first stage, the second stage, the third, the fourth? Which one? You're enlightened? What are you enlightened to?" It leaves them speechless. I pursue it: "You are a Buddha, and yet you can't even say what stage of fruition you have been certified to? How can you have jumped to Buddhahood?"

And yet they persist, claiming that not only are they themselves Buddhas, "Everybody is a Buddha." That is their theme. This is a great lie. When you haven't reached that state, you can't go shooting off your mouth. There's no one worse than a deviant teacher. Be careful not to become one, whether you understand the Buddhadharma or not. Don't be like one of them who was asked a point about the teachings and replied, "I'm getting old; I've forgotten." What did he mean he had forgotten? He never knew to begin with! That kind of talk is designed to cheat people. If you know, you say that you know. If you don't know, you should say you don't know. You can't say you've forgotten when you basically don't even understand what's being asked.

When deviant teachers propound their methods, they are intent upon taking advantage of situations, and the doctrines they explain are wrong. For instance, sexual desire is wrong, but they say it is fine. "It's the most wonderful activity." They praise it, causing people to become confused and to be unable to distinguish true principle. What is wrong, they say is right; what is right, they say is wrong. They have deviant knowledge and deviant views. Their outlook is improper. "During the Dharma-ending Age," Ananda says, "such teachers will abound."

I want to enable those beings to collect their thoughts and enter samadhi. Even though there will be as many deviant teachers in that age as there are sand grains in the Ganges, I still hope living beings will be able to give rise to proper knowledge and proper views. **How can I cause them to reside peacefully in a bodhimanda far from the exploits of demons, and be irreversible in their resolve for bodhi?** For example, there are some deviant demons and externalist religions that do nothing but cheat people with their teachings. They talk a lot about the affairs of men and women and say that the heavier one's sexual desire, the faster one can become a Buddha. This is totally wrong, entirely deviant! You should be attentive to this point. Don't be cheated by such people. In the orthodox dharma, any mention of sexual desire as favorable is wrong. Such methods of teaching are the exploits of demons.

Ananda wants to know how to help people of the final age not to retreat from bodhi. Some people study the Buddhadharma for a while and then go back on their resolve. "I don't want to study the Buddhadharma. It's too difficult. I have to get rid of all my faults. But what if I can't? It's better if I just don't study." They lose their vigor. They admit defeat. They are overcome by demonic ghosts. Ananda wants to know how to keep this from happening.

I2	The Thus Come One answers.
J1	He promises to speak; they wish to listen.

Sutra:

At that time, the World Honored One praised Ananda in front of the whole assembly, saying, "Good indeed! How good it is that you have asked how to establish a bodhimanda and to rescue and protect living beings who are sunk in the morass of the final age. Listen well, now, and I will tell you."

Ananda and the great assembly agreed to uphold the teaching.

Commentary:

Ananda said he wanted beings of the final age not to retreat from the resolve for bodhi. He wanted them to have decisive faith, to vow to protect and uphold the Buddhadharma, to study and practice the Buddhadharma, and never to go back on their resolve. But how could he get them to be that way? When Shakyamuni Buddha heard Ananda ask that question, he was delighted. The Buddha is in a state of unmoving suchness, but when someone wants to protect the Buddhadharma and help people become Buddhas, it nonetheless makes him happy. **At that time, the World Honored One praised Ananda in front of the whole assembly, saying, "Good indeed!"** The Buddha was pleased. "You're really fine, Ananda. **How good it is**" – he praises him twice – **"that you have asked how to establish a bodhimanda and to rescue and protect living beings who are sunk in the morass of the final age.** You want to help beings in the Dharma-ending Age who are being drowned in the water and consumed by the fire. **Listen well, now, and I will tell you."**

Ananda and the great assembly agreed to uphold the teaching. When they heard the Buddha agree to speak the dharma, their joy was even greater. The Buddha probably said, "Do you want to listen to this?"

Everyone undoubtedly answered, "We want to. We want to."

When deviant teachers explain their methods, their sole topic is sexual desire. The things they say are unprincipled. This should be distinguished clearly. Sometimes bodhisattvas also use compassion, kind words, and a protective heart to teach living beings, because they know that all living beings are steeped in desire. Every living being has thoughts of sexual desire. So he does not expect them to cut off their love and desire immediately, but he uses all kinds of expedient means to get them to see through and renounce sexual desire. Then they can put a stop to it themselves. This is the state of a bodhisattva, totally different from that of the deviant teachers of externalist ways.

Once, Guan Yin Bodhisattva transformed into a fishmonger. She was an exquisite woman who went about the village with her fish basket. No one in the village believed in the Buddha. But when the young men of the village caught sight of this maiden, they desired her. The village wasn't large, but there were at least a hundred young men there, and every one of them wanted to marry her. Guan Yin with the fish basket said, "There are so many of you! I can't marry a hundred men, but I've thought of a method to choose a husband. I will marry whichever of the hundred of you is the first to be able to learn to recite by heart the 'Universal Door Chapter' of the *Lotus Sutra*. Go back home and I'll give you three days."

But at the end of three days, there were forty or fifty who could recite it from memory. The woman with the fish basket said, "But there are still too many of you. Even though you have met the requirements, I can't have fifty husbands. This time go back and within five days memorize the *Vajra Sutra*. I'll marry whoever does that."

So the fifty who had made it to the first level went back and began to practice the *Vajra Sutra*. At the end of five days, there were some twenty who could recite it by heart. The fish monger said, "There are still too many of you. It's impossible for me to marry you all. I have one more task. Anyone who can memorize the

Lotus Sutra in seven days will be my husband. I believe whoever can do that will be worthy."

The twenty began to recite the *Lotus Sutra*, and at the end of seven days there was one man who could recite it from memory. His name was Ma, and he came from a wealthy family. So there was a large wedding and everyone was invited. That evening, after the festivities, they retired, but who would have guessed that the bride would have a heart attack and die suddenly? And the bridegroom had gone to so much effort! He had memorized the "Universal Door Chapter," the *Vajra Sutra*, and the *Lotus Sutra*, and still he had no bride. Shortly thereafter, the funeral took place, and a monk in purple robes appeared on the scene. "What's going on?" he asked.

"Our new daughter-in-law passed away suddenly, and we are burying her."

"No," said the monk. "There's nothing in that coffin at all! Who are you mourning for? Open it and take a look."

Indeed, the coffin was empty. They were all amazed. "Where had she gone? After her! Bring her back!"

The monk told them, "That was Guan Yin Bodhisattva. You people in this village didn't believe in the Buddha, so she manifested the appearance of a beautiful woman in order to get you young men, who are so fond of forms, to study the Buddhadharma. Then she left."

When the bridegroom, Ma, heard that, he renounced all worldly things and left the home-life. After that, he was certified to the fruition of a sage. That really happened in China.

J2   He brings up the three studies in general.

Sutra:

The Buddha told Ananda, "You constantly hear me explain in the vinaya that there are three unalterable aspects to cultivation. That is, collecting one's thoughts constitutes the precepts; from the precepts comes samadhi; and out of samadhi arises wisdom. Samadhi arises from precepts, and wisdom is

revealed out of samadhi. These are called the Three Non-Outflow Studies.

Commentary:

When everyone in the assembly had agreed to uphold the teaching, the Buddha told Ananda: **You constantly hear me explain in the vinaya that there are three unalterable aspects to cultivation.** The vinaya includes the rules for both the greater and lesser vehicles. It discusses the precepts. These three fixed aspects are unalterable. **That is, collecting one's thoughts constitutes the precepts.** These three are precepts, samadhi, and wisdom. You collect and maintain your thoughts, just as a magnet collects iron filings. This refers especially to our thoughts that "climb on conditions" – that take advantage of situations. When these thoughts take control, one is always paying attention to other people. One is continually thinking up ways to draw near to wealthy people or people in positions of authority. Such thoughts go on and on all day long. That's called "climbing on conditions"; it means that one has not collected one's thoughts. Collect those thoughts. Don't let them take advantage of situations. Don't let them run out at random. But our mind is such that it runs away with us, even if we don't want it to. We may forbid it to have false thinking, but in the next moment another false thought comes up. One ceases and the next one begins. The first thought dissolves, but the next one is already on its way. And before that one is completely gone, the next one has arisen. The mind that climbs on conditions never ceases. What you must do is to collect and maintain your thoughts. Bring your mind back to one point. The whole reason we can't become Buddhas, can't become enlightened, can't awaken to the Way, is that we do not have control of our mind. If you get your thoughts together, there is nothing you cannot do. You'll be successful at everything. The precepts, then, are designed to collect your thoughts. Precepts put a stop to evil and prevent further transgressions.

Samadhi arises from precepts. Holding precepts is like holding a bottle of muddy water still, until the silt settles and the water becomes clear. Samadhi means "not moving." **And wisdom is revealed out of samadhi.** As Manjushri Bodhisattva's verse said:

> When stillness is ultimate,
> the light penetrates.

You become enlightened. Within samadhi, your own genuine wisdom arises. **These are called the Three Non-outflow Studies.** Guard the precepts, and from the precepts will come samadhi. Out of samadhi will arise wisdom.

One Must Cut Off Lust

J3　He specifically lists the three studies.
K1　He lists the importance of the precepts first.
L1　He teaches him to hold precepts.
M1　He gathers in first and then gives evidence.
N1　One must cut off lust.
O1　Distinguishes the characteristic harm and benefit.
P1　First he explains the benefit or harm of holding or violating.
Q1　Holding it, then one certainly can get out of birth and death.

Sutra:

"**Ananda, why do I call collecting one's thoughts the precepts? If living beings in the six paths of any mundane world had no thoughts of lust, they would not have to follow a continual succession of births and deaths.**

Commentary:

Ananda, why do I call collecting one's thoughts the precepts? Now I will tell you. **If living beings in the six paths of any mundane world had no thoughts of lust**: the six paths include gods, humans, asuras, animals, hungry ghosts, and beings in the hells. If they were free of thoughts of sexual desire, **they would not have to follow a continual succession of births and deaths.** They could cut off birth and death.

| Q2 | Violating it, one certainly will fall into demonic paths. |

Sutra:

"Your basic purpose in cultivating is to transcend the wearisome defilements. But if you don't renounce your lustful thoughts, you will not be able to get out of the dust.

Commentary:

The Buddha is speaking to Ananda here when he says: **Your basic purpose in cultivating is to transcend the wearisome defilements.** You want to get out of birth and death. **But if you don't renounce your lustful thoughts, you will not be able to get out of the dust.** If you do not cut off sexual desire, it will be impossible to get out of the mundane defilements of the world. That's because thoughts of sexual desire are themselves defiling. They themselves are the wearisome dust. Not to speak of engaging in lustful practices, even the presence of such thoughts is unclean. If you don't renounce sexual desire, it's entirely unreasonable to hope to become enlightened and accomplish Buddhahood. To hold on to sexual desire on the one hand and expect to become enlightened on the other is the stupidest kind of thinking. People who think that way are impossible to teach. Even if Shakyamuni Buddha himself appeared in the world right now, he would have no way to bring such people to attainment of fruition. Such people are the most dull-witted of all.

Sutra:

"Even though one may have some wisdom and the manifestation of Chan samadhi, one is certain to enter demonic paths if one does not cut off lust. At best, one will be a demon king; on the average, one will be in the retinue of demons; at the lowest level, one will be a female demon.

Commentary:

Even though one may have some wisdom and the manifestation of Chan samadhi, one is certain to enter demonic paths if one does not cut off lust. You may be wise, and when you sit down to meditate you may experience light ease and feel extremely comfortable – that is, you can enter Chan samadhi. You think you're wise, then? If you don't put a stop to lust, you'll end up a demon! **At best, one will be a demon king** in the sixth desire heaven. **On the average, one will be in the retinue of demons.** One will become an ordinary demon. **At the lowest level, one will be a female demon.** They are beautiful, but extremely coarse. People with wisdom should be careful. Smart people should take careful note of this passage. Don't let your intelligence go back on you so that you make a mistake in the end. Don't have the attitude: "You don't understand, but I do. You're not clear, but I am." That's petty intelligence, petty wisdom. Don't let a promising future go to ruin.

Sutra:

"**These demons have their groups of disciples. Each says of himself that he has accomplished the Unsurpassed Way.**

Commentary:

These people with a little wisdom who do not cut off their lust are always talking about love and desire. "I love you, you love me," and they love back and forth until they become demonic. Then what happens? **These demons have their groups of disciples. Each says of himself that he has accomplished the Unsurpassed Way.** They, too, will have disciples and protectors. Totally without shame, they will loudly pronounce that they have achieved the highest path. "I'm a Buddha! We are all supreme and unsurpassed!" Basically such people are demons, but they don't admit to it; they profess instead to be Buddhas. You see, there are even phony Buddhas. But they don't see themselves as phony; they think they are for real. They believe:

> In heaven above, on earth below
> I alone am honored.

P2	He discusses the behavior of demons within Buddhism.
Q1	Greed for lust turns the world.

Sutra:

"**After my extinction, in the Dharma-ending Age, these hordes of demons will abound, spreading like wildfire as they openly practice greed and lust.** Claiming to be good knowing advisors, they will cause living beings to fall into the pit of love and views and lose the way to bodhi."

Commentary:

Shakyamuni Buddha said, "While I'm in the world, such demons will not dare to show themselves, but **after my extinction, in the Dharma-ending Age, these hordes of demons will abound.**" It is just our present age that is being referred to here, when the dharma is about to die out. There are simply too many of these demons around, going about everywhere discussing sexual desire. And they themselves revel in lust, be they men or women. At the same time, they think that they are enlightened and have become Buddhas.

How is it that I recognize such people as these, such as the one who says he's a Buddha – we won't mention any names. He said he was a Buddha, and I said he was a demon.

"Who's a demon!?" he said.

"You are," I replied. How did I know? He's just like what's described here. He's always talking about emotion and love. "Love, love. I love everybody!" It's really shameless. What right do you have to be in love with everyone? These demons abound, **spreading like wildfire as they openly practice greed and lust.** They'll be all the rage in the world. Ignorant people will be taken in by them, thinking what they have to say makes sense. It will especially agree with young people's way of thinking. As the saying goes, "Persons of similar (atrocious) tastes get together." They praise one another as they go down this road. If they didn't agree with each other's ideas, they wouldn't do that. If people's paths are not in agreement, they won't collaborate with one another.

But if their thinking is the same, then the blind can lead the blind. How pitiful! I'm not scolding people here, but

> If one who is dazed
> transmits the delusion to another,
> When all is said and done,
> neither one understands.
> The teacher falls into the hells,
> And the disciples burrow in after him.

The teacher winds up in the hells, and when his disciples show up there as well, he is surprised. "How did you get here? This is a terrible place!"

"You came first, and you're our teacher, so of course we would follow you," they reply.

Claiming to be good knowing advisors. They boast, "I give lectures all over the place to lots of people." Ridiculous! **They will cause living beings to fall into the pit of love and views and lose the Way to bodhi.** They cause all they come in contact with to fall into the pit of sexual desire. They forfeit bodhi and end up in the hells.

Q2 Teaching people to cut off lust is the Buddha's instruction.

Sutra:

"When you teach people in the world to cultivate samadhi, they must first of all sever the mind of lust. This is the first clear and unalterable instruction on purity given by the Thus Come Ones and the Buddhas of the past, World Honored Ones.

Commentary:

Demon kings advocate love. The difference between that and the teaching of a bodhisattva is ever so slight – like the flip of a hand. In what way is it different? Bodhisattvas also love people, but their love is a compassionate and protective kind, devoid of sexual desire. But there is a current of lust that runs through everything a demon king says. He openly advocates it, to the point that he says that the heavier one's sexual desire, the higher the level of enlightenment one can reach. This kind of deviant doctrine harms people. Bodhisattvas have no lust; they do not make distinctions between living beings and themselves. Demons have motives; they are greedy for things. Bodhisattvas have no ulterior motives and are not greedy. In regard to this, the Buddha's teaching explains the twelve links of conditioned causation.

When you teach people in the world to cultivate samadhi, they must first of all sever the mind of lust. Teach them to cut off their thoughts of sexual desire. **This is the first clear and unalterable instruction on purity given by the Thus Come Ones and the Buddhas of the past, World Honored Ones.** This is the method of teaching used by the Thus Come Ones. It is the resolution of all the Buddhas of the past. This is clear instruction that teaches people how to be pure. One must cut off lust. This is a fixed principle. It is not the least bit flexible. It's not to say that one can have lust or not have it. One must get rid of it. If you want to be enlightened and also hold on to your thoughts of lust, then you certainly will join the retinue of demons.

P3 Decides if the bodhimanda can be accomplished.
Q1 An analogy shows that if one doesn't cut off lust, bodhi can't be obtained.

Sutra:

"**Therefore, Ananda, if cultivators of Chan samadhi do not cut off lust, they will be like someone who cooks sand in the hope of getting rice. After hundreds of thousands of aeons, it will still be just hot sand. Why? It wasn't rice to begin with; it was only sand.**

Commentary:

You see, now he brings up an analogy. He tells Ananda, "You don't believe it, so I'll explain the principle for you. **Therefore, Ananda, if cultivators of Chan samadhi do not cut off lust, they will be like someone who cooks sand in the hope of getting rice.**" If one does not sever sexual desire and yet cultivates and meditates every day, then one will cultivate on the one hand, and have outflows on the other. Everything one gains will be dissipated. Whatever one gains in cultivation will be lost tenfold in outflows; if one cultivates ten times as much, one will lose a hundred times as much in outflows. Unable to renounce sexual desire, one still sits in meditation with the hope of getting enlightened, with the aim of getting a little upside-down bliss. This is just like cooking sand in the hope of getting rice. **After hundreds of thousands of aeons, it will still be just hot sand.** It's useless. **Why? It wasn't rice to begin with; it was only sand.** You expect to become enlightened without giving up sexual desire? It's the same as expecting to get rice from sand.

There's something else to be said here. If you can sever sexual desire, then even if you are together with the opposite sex all day long, there will be no problem. There won't be any sexual desire, any appearance of male or female, any appearance of people, of self, of living beings, or of a lifespan. Some people know no shame and say, "That's the way I am." To just say you're that way isn't enough. There's no proof. How do you know you're that way? If you were that way, you basically wouldn't recognize that you were. You couldn't have the idea that you didn't have any sexual desire. If you don't, you simply don't. You wouldn't go around advertising it. That just shows that you really aren't that way. If you really don't have any sexual desire, then

> The eyes see forms appear,
>   but inside there is nothing.
> The ears hear defiling sounds,
>   but the mind does not know of them.

No matter how pleasing a sound the ear picks up, your mind is unaware of it. Then you've got a little going for you. And then if you can reach the point that you can walk, sit, and lie down together with someone of the opposite sex without there being any incident – any arisal of thoughts of sexual desire – and really have there be none – that will count. It's not to say that your mind still races but you grit your teeth and say firmly, "I can take it." That doesn't count. It has to be that not one thought arises – the mind does not move, that there basically is no trace of lust in your heart. That's genuine. If you occasionally are still aware of what women are all about, then you've failed the test.

Once there was someone who got enlightened and went to seek certification from his teacher. "What enlightenment have you opened?" his teacher asked.

His reply was, "Oh, before I never realized it, but now I know that bhikshunis are women." His teacher checked him out with the buddha eye and saw that indeed he was enlightened. "You're all right," he said in certification.

"Who doesn't know that?" you say.

If you weren't enlightened, you wouldn't even say that much. It was because he had awakened that he voiced that observation. This is not something you can cheat people with – especially since his teacher had the buddha eye open. He looked at him and knew that he had realized the first fruition of arhatship.

Sutra:

"If you seek the Buddha's wonderful fruition and still have physical lust, then even if you attain a wonderful awakening, it will be based in lust. With lust at the source, you will revolve in the three paths and not be able to get out. Which road will you take to cultivate and be certified to the Thus Come One's nirvana?

Commentary:

The Buddha said to Ananda, "Your fondness for Matangi's daughter not only involved thoughts of lust; you still had physical lust, as well. **If you see the Buddha's wonderful fruition and still have physical lust, then even if you attain a wonderful awakening, it will be based in lust.** Although you may attain the subtle principles at the heart of it, you still have not gotten rid of the roots of lust. **With lust at the source, you will revolve in the three paths and not be able to get out.** In the future you will certainly fall into the hells." The "three paths" are those of animals, hungry ghosts, and beings in the hells. And you will just revolve in these three and be unable to leave them. **Which road will you take to cultivate and be certified to the Thus Come One's nirvana?** Which of these paths will lead you to that fruition?

Q2 Diligently and profoundly cutting off lust can bring accomplishment.

Sutra:

"**You must cut off the lust which is intrinsic in both body and mind. Then get rid of even the aspect of cutting it off. At that point you have some hope of attaining the Buddha's bodhi.**

Commentary:

You must cut off the lust which is intrinsic in both body and mind. You definitely must get rid of the most subtle and fine, the most infinitesimal single thought of lust. That just means that ignorance itself must go. It must be done both physically and mentally. **Then get rid of even the aspect of cutting it off.** You cannot even be aware of having cut it off. **At that point you have some hope of attaining the Buddha's bodhi.**

O2 He speaks of the divisions of deviant and proper.

Sutra:

"**What I have said here is the Buddha's teaching. Any explanation counter to it is the teaching of Papiyan.**

Commentary:

What I have said here is the Buddha's teaching. This is the way the Buddhas explain the dharma. **Any explanation counter to it is the teaching of Papiyan**, methods taught by a demon king. "Papiyan" is a Sanskrit term that means "evil one" and refers to Mara, the demon king.

People who come to listen to the sutras must certainly be able to see. The blind cannot come to hear the sutras, nor can the deaf or dumb. The more the people come to hear, the smarter they get. Everyone should open his eye of genuine wisdom and truly turn the organ of the ear back to the self-nature. Do not seek outside.

One Must Cut Off Killing

N2 One must cut off killing.
O1 He distinguishes the characteristic harm and benefit.
P1 First he explains the benefit or harm of holding or violating.
Q1 Holding it, then one certainly can get out of birth and death.

Sutra:

"**Further, Ananda, if living beings in the six paths of any mundane world had no thoughts of killing, they would not have to follow a continual succession of births and deaths.**

Commentary:

If gods, humans, asuras, animals, hungry ghosts, and hell-dwellers did not harbor thoughts of killing, but instead ceased killing and liberated the living, they could get out of birth and death. Here the reference is to mere thoughts of killing, not to mention acts of killing. If one ceases killing, one does not have to undergo rebirth in the six paths and be subject to the karma that accompanies the process of birth and death.

Q2 Violating it, one certainly will fall into the path of spirits.

Sutra:

"**Your basic purpose in cultivating samadhi is to transcend the wearisome defilements. But if you do not renounce your thoughts of killing, you will not be able to get out of the dust.**

Commentary:

Ananda, you want to cultivate samadhi power. **Your basic purpose in cultivating samadhi is to transcend the wearisome defilements.** Your hope from the beginning has been to get out of the mundane dust. **But if you do not renounce your thoughts of killing, you will not be able to get out of the dust.** How can one get rid of thoughts of killing? Cease killing and liberate the living. Above, the text says, "If you do not renounce your lustful thoughts, you cannot get out of the dust." You must sever thoughts of sexual desire in order to be free of defilements. That's the only way you can transcend the cycle of rebirth in the six paths. But if you dispense with your thoughts of lust and still harbor thoughts of killing, you still cannot get out of the mundane world. You cannot transcend rebirth.

Sutra:

"Even though one may have some wisdom and the manifestation of Chan samadhi, one is certain to enter the path of spirits if one does not cease killing. At best, a person will become a mighty ghost; on the average, one will become a flying yaksha, a ghost leader, or the like; at the lowest level, one will become an earth-bound rakshasa.

Commentary:

Even though one may have some wisdom and the manifestation of Chan samadhi, one is certain to enter the path of spirits if one does not cease killing. "Wisdom" here refers to worldly intelligence and skill in debate, not to transcendental wisdom. It is an ordinary kind of wisdom that enables one to have a certain amount of eloquence. And even if you have cultivated to the point that you have *gong fu* in Chan – you've had some responses – still, if you don't get rid of thoughts of killing, you'll fall into the realm of spirits. This means you might become a ruling god in the heavens. **At best, a person will become a mighty ghost,** that is, a powerful heavenly general. **On the average, one will become a flying yaksha.** The mighty ghosts are heaven-traveling yakshas;

the flying yakshas travel in space. Or one will become **a ghost leader, or the like.** One will be a ghost who commands other ghosts. **At the lowest level, one will be an earth-bound rakshasa.**

Sutra:

"These ghosts and spirits have their groups of disciples. Each says of himself that he has accomplished the Unsurpassed Way.

Commentary:

The ruling gods, the mighty ghosts in the heavens, the yakshas and rakshasas in the human realm, and the ghosts in the hells also have a lot of followers. There are rich ghosts, ghosts with a little wealth, and poor ghosts. There are tens of thousands of varieties of ghosts. Guan Di Gong in China is an example of a wealthy ghost. But after he took refuge with the Buddha, he came to be known as Qie Lan Bodhisattva, a dharma-protecting spirit. In the Buddha's assembly he must stand; he has no seat assignment. However, the ghosts referred to here claim to have attained the Supreme Way.

P2　He discusses the behavior of demons within Buddhism.
Q1　Eating flesh turns the world into a teaching by ghosts.

Sutra:

"After my extinction, in the Dharma-ending Age, these hordes of ghosts and spirits will abound, spreading like wildfire as they argue that eating meat will bring one to the bodhi way.

Commentary:

After my extinction, in the Dharma-ending Age, these hordes of ghosts and spirits will abound. That's the present time he's talking about – the age that you and I live in. There are innumerable ghosts and spirits in this Dharma-ending Age, all because in former lives they could not stop killing. They practiced cultivation, but could not cease killing, and so they fell into the path of the spirits. In the Dharma-ending Age, these beings will be **spreading like wildfire as they argue that eating meat will bring one to the bodhi way.** They say, "I eat meat and I've become a

Buddha just the same. I didn't have to stop killing or eat vegetarian food, but I'm enlightened and have attained the bodhi way, that is, I am a Buddha." This is like a certain person who claims to be enlightened but who eats meat, drinks alcohol, smokes cigarettes, and has a group of young followers that he teaches to smoke marijuana and take LSD. Who has ever heard of someone enlightened behaving like that? When the Buddha himself became enlightened, he did not use such dope. Now you take pills that poison your system, upset your energy balance, and bring you to the brink of death, and you still insist you are enlightened. Is that upside-down or not? I ask you.

Sutra:

"Ananda, I permit the bhikshus to eat five kinds of pure meat. This meat is actually a transformation brought into being by my spiritual powers. It basically has no life-force. You brahmans live in a climate so hot and humid, and on such sandy and rocky land, that vegetables will not grow; therefore, I have had to assist you with spiritual powers and compassion. Because of the magnitude of this kindness and compassion, what you eat that tastes like meat is merely said to be meat; in fact, however, it is not. After my extinction, how can those who eat the flesh of living beings be called the disciples of Shakya?

Commentary:

Ananda, I permit the bhikshus to eat five kinds of pure meat. The Buddha's teaching allows these five kinds:

1) Flesh of an animal that I did not see killed.
2) Flesh of an animal that I did not hear killed.
3) Flesh of an animal that I am sure was not killed for my sake.
4) Flesh of an animal that died by itself.
5) Flesh that is the leavings of an animal after birds have scavenged.

This meat is actually a transformation brought into being by my spiritual powers. It basically has no life-force. The Buddha created these kinds of flesh; they are not from living creatures. They have no life-force; that is, no consciousness, no temperature, and no breath. **You brahmans live in a climate so hot and humid, and on such sandy and rocky land, that vegetables will not grow.** You who practice pure conduct live in a land full of sand and dampness. **Therefore, I have had to assist you with spiritual powers and compassion. Because of the magnitude of this kindness and compassion, what you eat that tastes like meat is merely said to be meat; in fact, however, it is not.** That's what you are really eating. I allow you to eat this kind of meat at present. But, **after my extinction, how can those who eat the flesh of living beings be called the disciples of Shakya?** They are not eating the five kinds of pure meat; they are just eating the flesh of living beings outright. Are they to be known as disciples of the Buddha? They cannot be referred to as disciples of Shakya, that is, people who left the home life.

Sutra:

"**You should know that these people who eat meat may gain some awareness and may seem to be in samadhi, but they are all great rakshasas. When their retribution ends, they are bound to sink into the bitter sea of birth and death. They are not disciples of the Buddha. Such people as these kill and eat one another in a never-ending cycle. How can such people transcend the triple realm?**

Commentary:

You should know that these people who eat meat may gain some awareness and may seem to be in samadhi, but they are all great rakshasas. They pay no attention to what kind of flesh they are eating. They don't care whether it is one of the three kinds of pure meat or the five kinds of pure meat; if it's meat, they'll eat it. Ananda, you should realize that after my extinction such beings will pretend to be disciples of the Buddha and will consume both alcohol and meat. They'll be completely uninhibited, saying that everyone is free to do as he or she pleases. Although they may attain a small state of awakening or gain a little wisdom, they will only appear to be in samadhi. Actually they are not. They are like the person who came here and claimed he was the same as the Sixth Patriarch.

"What evidence do you have that you are the same?" I asked him.

He replied, "I don't have any evidence that I'm not the same." He thought that was a wise answer. Actually, he was in a class with the beings described in this passage. Such people may seem to have a little samadhi power, but in fact they are great rakshasas – big demons, big ghosts.

When their retribution ends, they are bound to sink into the bitter sea of birth and death. They are not disciples of the Buddha. Although such people wear the Buddha's clothes and eat the Buddha's food, they are not disciples of the Buddha. **Such people as these kill and eat one another in a never-ending cycle.** They take life and eat meat and do not prohibit either one. They keep eating one another; you eat me, and I eat you; kill and eat, be killed and eaten. **How can such people transcend the triple realm?** Behavior like this sets up an endless cycle. In this life, you eat my flesh; and in the next life, I eat yours. In the life after that, it's your turn to eat me again, and it goes on and on. How can such beings get out of the desire realm, the form realm, and the formless realm?

Q2 Teaching people to cut off killing is the Buddha's instruction.

Sutra:

"When you teach people in the world to cultivate samadhi, they must also cut off killing. This is the second clear and unalterable instruction on purity given by the Thus Come Ones and the Buddhas of the past, World Honored Ones.

Commentary:

When you teach people in the world to cultivate samadhi, they must also cut off killing. First, they must cut off sexual desire; they must also sever their thoughts of killing. **This is the second clear and unalterable instruction on purity given by the Thus Come One and the Buddhas of the past, World Honored Ones.** This is the teaching advocated by the Buddha. Both the Buddhas of the past and the Buddhas of the present teach this second clear and fixed instruction on purity. You must certainly revere it. If you don't, you won't be able to get out of the triple realm.

P3 He decides if liberation can be obtained.
Q1 An analogy makes clear, if one doesn't cut off killing it is difficult to get free.

Sutra:

"Therefore, Ananda, if cultivators of Chan samadhi do not cut off killing, they are like one who stops up his ears and calls out in a loud voice, expecting no one to hear him. It is to wish to hide what is completely evident.

Commentary:

Therefore, Ananda, if cultivators of Chan samadhi do not cut off killing, they sever their compassionate seeds. Once they have lost their sense of compassion, **they are like one who stops up his ears and calls out in a loud voice, expecting no one to hear him.** This is known as plugging up one's ears while one steals a bell; one supposes that if one can't hear oneself, no one else can either. **It is to wish to hide what is completely evident.** The more one wishes to cover up one's conduct, the more it is revealed. In the same way, someone who practices samadhi but does not stop killing will find it impossible to realize his expectations.

Sutra:

"Bodhisattvas and bhikshus who practice purity will not even step on grass in the pathway; even less will they pull it up with their hand. How can one with great compassion pick up the flesh and blood of living beings and proceed to eat his fill?

Commentary:

Bodhisattvas and bhikshus who practice purity until their conduct is extremely pure and lofty, **will not even step on grass in the pathway.** At a place where several paths come together there is usually grass growing in the walkway. A pure bhikshu or bodhisattva will not walk on growing grass. It could kill the grass. **Even less will they pull it up with their hand.** They don't do any weeding. **How can one with great compassion pick up the flesh and blood of living beings and proceed to eat his fill?** That is not permissible.

Q2 If one diligently and profoundly cuts off killing, one can get free.

Sutra:

"**Bhikshus who do not wear silk, leather boots, furs, or down from this country, or consume milk, cream, or butter can truly transcend this world. When they have paid back their past debts, they will not have to re-enter the triple realm.**

Commentary:

Bhikshus who do not wear silk, leather boots, furs, or down from this country, or consume milk, cream, or butter can truly transcend the world. Silk, leather, furs, and down come from living creatures. The life of the creature must be taken in order to make these things. Ordinary cotton is not included here. Therefore, they don't wear leather shoes or carry leather bags. Nor do they use milk products. **When they have paid back their past debts, they will not have to re-enter the triple realm.** It says here that milk and milk products should not be ingested, but in the precepts of the greater and lesser vehicles it does not state that one must certainly refrain from these things. This passage of sutra text is describing those who hold precepts with a maximum of purity. They thoroughly uphold the precept against killing. They do not use anything that has any connection with living creatures. They don't wear silk because a lot of silkworms' lives must be spent in the process of obtaining the silk. They don't eat honey, because it is made from bees. But in the vinaya proper this is an open question.

There is room for flexibility. The precepts do not specifically forbid these things. For you to avoid using them is to be extremely pure. It is very good.

Sutra:

"**Why? It is because when one wears something taken from a living creature, one creates conditions with it, just as when people eat the hundred grains, their feet cannot leave the earth. Both physically and mentally one must avoid the bodies and the by-products of living beings, by neither wearing them nor eating them. I say that such people have true liberation.**

Commentary:

Why? It is because when one wears something taken from a living creature, one creates conditions with it. For example, when you wear silk, you have a connection with the worms that made it. If you don't want to be that kind of creature, you should sever connections with it. It is **just as when people eat the hundred grains, their feet cannot leave the earth.** The first people on earth were actually heavenly beings that came down from the Great Brahma Heaven. This happened in the past when the fire of the kalpa raged over the earth until it had destroyed all signs of people. Afterward there began a barren period which extended for one knows not how long. And then, one day some heavenly beings flew down from the Brahma Heaven and alighted on earth. By this time, the earth was covered with a special something that looked quite good. They picked some and found it to be fragrant as well. So they ate it. Once they ate this "fat of the land," they could no longer fly. They couldn't mount the clouds and drive the fog. No longer mobile, they stood on earth and called out to their brothers and sisters who happened by in space. These heavenly beings landed and also partook of the "fat of the land," and so they too became earth-bound. They couldn't go back to the heavens; and that's how the human race came to be on earth. Some people hold that we came from monkeys. But if that's the case, what keeps us from turning back into monkeys? In fact, it all started when the heavenly beings came down to earth. As the number of people increased, the fat of the land was entirely consumed, and that whole species of plant died out. Then they had to eat "the hundred grains."

They are:

1. twenty varieties of rice,
2. twenty varieties of millet,
3. twenty varieties of beans,
4. twenty varieties of vegetables,
5. twenty varieties of melons.

There were more or less twenty kinds of each, making a hundred varieties in all. Once they ate them, "their feet couldn't leave the earth." We ascribe it to gravity, but the reason behind it is that people consume this kind of food.

Both physically and mentally one must avoid the bodies and by-products of living beings, by neither wearing them nor eating them. We people want to keep our bodies and minds free from karma created in connection with the bodies of other living creatures or with anything that comes from them. One cannot physically take life, nor can one do so mentally. One should not wear anything connected with the life of another being or eat the flesh of their bodies. **I say that such people have true liberation.** They have really become free.

O2 He speaks of the division into deviant and proper.

Sutra:

"What I have said here is the Buddha's teaching. Any explanation counter to it is the teaching of Papiyan.

Commentary:

What I have said here is the Buddha's teaching. My explanation is the dharma spoken by the Buddhas of the ten directions and the three periods of time. **Any explanation counter to it is the teaching of Papiyan.** Any doctrine that agrees with my principle is the teaching that the Buddhas speak. Any theory that disagrees with the principles I have explained here is the talk of a demon king.

Now that you are hearing the *Shurangama Sutra*, you can use it as a freak-spotting mirror. If someone is pretending to be a person and you shine the mirror on him, he will be revealed in his true form – a weirdo. Perhaps he's a pig-spirit or a cow-spirit or a horse-spirit or a mountain essence or water-monster. Maybe it's a ghost king. Whatever it might be, the mirror will show it up. Now that you've heard the *Shurangama Sutra*, you will be able to know whether someone is giving proper instructions by comparing it to what is told in this sutra. So it is like a freak-spotting mirror. That's why I said earlier that the blind, deaf, and dumb have no chance to hear my explanation of the sutra. The deaf basically can't hear it, but here I'm not referring to people who are physically deaf, but to people who hear the dharma and yet are deaf to it. Mutes also miss the point when I lecture. I hope that all of you who are able to hear the *Shurangama Sutra* will become good knowing advisors in the future; that you will come to genuinely understand the Buddhadharma. Then you can teach the blind, deaf, and mute. When you lecture, you can use an amplifying system, and then even though they are outside, they will be able to hear and will no longer be deaf or mute. People who don't understand the Buddhadharma are most pitiful. So, when you have mastered the Buddhadharma, you should go teach it to others. That means that at this stage you should pay special attention as you study.

One Must Cut Off Stealing

N3 One must cut off stealing.
O1 He distinguishes the characteristic harm and benefit.
P1 First he discusses the benefit or harm of holding or violating.
Q1 Holding it, one then certainly can get out of birth and death.

Sutra:

"**Further, Ananda, if living beings in the six paths of any mundane world had no thoughts of stealing, they would not have to follow a continuous succession of births and deaths.**

Commentary:

The Buddha again calls out to Ananda: **Further, Ananda, if living beings in the six paths of any mundane world had no thoughts of stealing, they would not have to follow a continuous succession of births and deaths.** The gods, people, animals, hungry ghosts, and hell-dwellers would not steal, even in their minds. They wouldn't steal anything whatsoever, be it visible or invisible, valuable or worthless. Not only not actually taking it, but not even having the thought of taking it arises in one's mind: that is what is meant by not stealing. If they could refrain from stealing as well as from lust and killing, they wouldn't get involved in the continuity of birth and death, and they would also be free of the continuity of karmic retribution and from the continuity of the world.

Q2 Violating it, one certainly will fall into deviant paths.

Sutra:

"**Your basic purpose in cultivating samadhi is to transcend the wearisome defilements. But if you do not renounce your thoughts of stealing, you will not be able to get out of the dust.**

Commentary:

Your basic purpose in cultivating samadhi is to transcend the wearisome defilements. You want to develop proper concentration. Your original reason for this was to get out of the cycle of rebirths in the mundane world. But, if you still have ideas about stealing things, **but if you do not renounce your thoughts of stealing, you will not be able to get out of the dust.** "Dust" refers to the burning house of the triple realm.

Sutra:

"**Even though one may have some wisdom and the manifestation of Chan samadhi, one is certain to enter a devious path if one does not cease stealing. At best, one will be an apparition; on the average, one will become a phantom; at the lowest level, one will be a devious person who is possessed by a mei ghost.**

Commentary:

Even though one may have some wisdom and the manifestation of Chan samadhi, one is certain to enter a devious path if one does not cease stealing. Basically, this kind of person has no genuine wisdom, for if he did, he would not steal, nor would he lust, nor would he kill. It's just because he lacks genuine wisdom that he does these things. But let us allow that someone like this has a little wisdom and is just a trifle smarter than the average person, and when he sits he slips into an oblivion that's more or less like samadhi. Yet, this person thinks that he has achieved some incredible state which no one else has ever come close to. He feels he has skill which surpasses everyone else's. His views are arrogant, and if he doesn't stop stealing, he will fall into a devious path. Even with a little wisdom and a little samadhi, one will fall into an improper state of being because of stealing. On this devious path, one will teach others ways which are dark and incorrect. One will teach people deviant knowledge and deviant views. **At best, one will be an apparition.** When you see such a being, he appears to be extremely intelligent; but, in fact, he is false. In the Chinese text *The Nature of Medicine*, there is mention of herbs endowed with this essence, but, in fact, the essence is not real. **On the average, one will become a phantom,** a strange being who possesses spiritual powers and can harm people. **At the lowest level, one will be a devious person who is possessed by a mei ghost.** You remember that the kumbhanda was a mei ghost who could cause paralysis in a person during sleep. The kind of ghost mentioned here takes over a person who is awake and manipulates his body, mouth, and mind for its own purposes. It speaks through the person and can gain complete control of him.

These people are what are known as mediums, or they can sometimes become sorcerers or exorcists. In America, I encountered a person like this, an American who said he was Jesus. A minute later he would announce that God had come upon him to speak. Then, after a time he would announce that Jesus had come and wanted to talk to him. It was about five years ago when he came to see me. I scolded him. I said, "You don't even recognize yourself. You are a demonic ghost through and through, and you are up to no good." He didn't like the phrase "demonic ghost," so he left. He came to discuss doctrine with me, but he never returned after I scolded him. And I thought to myself, "I don't know how to talk to people. Why did I scare away that 'Jesus-God'?" Anyway, that's an example of this kind of devious person. Why do they have that kind of karmic retribution? It is because in former lives they stole things, and so they are bound to fall into one of these three categories.

Sometimes in China these mediums were pretty spectacular. They could stick a knife in the crown of their heads and yet not die. The spirit possessing them would remove the blade by the use of a mantra in such a way that the person didn't even bleed. Some would pound nails into their shoulders, and from the nails they would hang several swords weighing more than ten pounds each. They could hang four of them and then spin them. It was awesome to watch. People were terrified. Sometimes they were really talented. I've seen a lot of these devious demons and adherents of externalist ways. When you look into the *Shurangama Sutra*, you realize that long ago the Buddha described all the different kinds of beings in the world very clearly. Therefore, having heard the *Shurangama Sutra*, you should be able to recognize whatever you come up against.

This section is called the "four clear and unalterable instructions on purity," and it is an extremely important passage of this sutra. So pay close attention.

If one can't stop stealing, one will find it impossible to become a Buddha, however much one hopes to become one. Now that we understand this doctrine, people who do steal should change. Those who don't should not let thoughts of stealing arise. That is how to be most in accord with the Way.

Sutra:

"These devious hordes have their groups of disciples. Each says of himself that he has accomplished the Unsurpassed Way.

Commentary:

These devious hordes are phantoms, demons, ghosts, and weird beings, and the *li*, *mei*, and *wang liang* ghosts that harm people. They all **have their groups of disciples.** In this world, every category of being has its followers. As it says,

> The good gather together;
> The bad form gangs;
> People find people who are like themselves.

So, even these devious ghosts and demons mass together and have their devotees. **Each says of himself that he has accomplished the Unsurpassed Way.** They do not recognize what is truly supreme, but instead contend that their way of doing things is the best. They say they have attained the highest way possible, even to the point that they take the Buddha's name in vain and say that's what they are. "Just take a look at the magnitude of my spiritual powers," they argue. But, in fact, they are phantoms, demons, ghosts, and weird beings. They are thoroughly improper in their conduct.

P2 He discusses the behavior of weird beings within Buddhism.
Q1 Hidden influences are the teachings of weird beings.

Sutra:

"After my extinction, in the Dharma-ending Age, these phantoms and apparitions will abound, spreading like wildfire as they surreptitiously cheat others. Calling themselves good knowing advisors, they will each say that they have attained the superhuman abilities. Enticing and deceiving the ignorant, or frightening them out of their wits, they disrupt and lay waste to households wherever they go.

Commentary:

I've met very many of these demonic ghosts. Westerners may not be too familiar with these strange things, but it's not just that they come to be because Chinese people believe in ghosts and spirits. It's just that, as time goes on, the strange phenomena that appear in the world become more numerous.

After my extinction, in the Dharma-ending Age, these phantoms and apparitions will abound. Shakyamuni Buddha is telling us here that the age we live in will be plagued with such deviant creatures. We people shouldn't have to see things for ourselves to believe they exist. There are simply too many things in the world which one will never see. If we had to wait until we had seen each and every one of them with our own eyes, we wouldn't be done looking in this lifetime. There are some things you just have to take others' word for. They spread **like wildfire as they surreptitiously cheat others.** They will be like a fire that literally burns people up. People who don't recognize these devious beings will fall in with them and it will be just as if they had stepped into a raging fire. The person will be burned. "Secret and hidden" means they will go about cheating others.

Calling themselves good knowing advisors, they will each say that they have attained the superhuman abilities. They will speak of themselves as bright-eyed good knowing advisors. "Superhuman" refers to a bodhisattva. In other words, they will say they are bodhisattvas. In Buddhism, even though you are a bodhisattva, or even a Buddha who has come again, you cannot say that you are a Buddha or a bodhisattva. You must keep silent about it so long as you live, down to your last breath. "I'm a Buddha!" "I'm a bodhisattva!" "I'm an arhat!" You cannot speak like that. Anyone who speaks like that is a demonic ghost, just like the ones being described here. When can you let it be known? After you die. Then people ought to know. But you cannot let people know who you are before you die. What meaning would there be in your announcing that you are a Buddha? What meaning? You say you are a bodhisattva? Why? What is your meaning in saying so? There could be no other reason than to get people to believe in you. And why would you want people to believe in you? So they will give you money. You do it to take advantage of situations and climb on conditions. If that's not your intent, then why would you be telling people you are a living Buddha? If you are a bodhisattva, fine, you're a bodhisattva; what would you be doing telling people so?

That reminds me of something that happened once in China. An official once went to Guo Qing monastery on Tian Tai mountain to ask questions of the Abbot Feng Kan. The official and the abbot chatted. What was the official's name, you wonder? Don't ask me; I've forgotten. Perhaps it was you, or perhaps it was me; it's not for certain. The official said to the abbot, "In the past, there used to be a lot of bodhisattvas who came into the world, but there aren't any in this day and age. I'd like to meet a genuine bodhisattva, but I can't find one."

Abbot Feng Kan said, "Oh, you want to see a bodhisattva? We have two here. I'll introduce you to them, and you can go see them."

The official was duly surprised, "Two bodhisattvas, right here? You mean ones made of clay, or carved wooden ones?"

"No," replied the abbot. "These two are flesh-body bodhisattvas. They are living bodhisattvas."

"No kidding?" asked the official.

"I'm the abbot here. Would I joke with you about a thing like that?"

"Who are they?"

"One is the cook and the other boils the water. One is named Han Shan and the other is named Shi De. One is a transformation of Manjushri Bodhisattva, and the other is a transformation of Universal Worthy (Samantabhadra) Bodhisattva. They practice ascetic practices in this temple, doing menial tasks. They do the things that no one else likes to do. If you want to see them, it's quite simple. Just go to the kitchen and you'll find them there."

The official asked the guest prefect to take him to the kitchen. There they found two grimy, tattered monks with long hair and beards, dirty faces, and a generally disreputable appearance. But the abbot had said these two were bodhisattvas, and so he dared not look down on them. Instead, he bowed to them.

"What are you doing?" the two demanded. "Why are you bowing to us?"

"Abbot Feng Kan said you were transformations of Manjushri and Universal Worthy Bodhisattvas, so of course I'm bowing to you."

"Feng Kan's flapped his tongue" – by which they meant he was a busybody. "He's said too much this time." So, as the official bowed, they backed up and backed up and backed up, one knows not how great a distance – probably several hundred steps from the kitchen to the rock cliff at the base of the mountain. Then they said, "Feng Kan has flapped his tongue. You didn't even bow to Amitabha. What are you doing bowing to us?"

"Who's Amitabha?" asked the official.

"The abbot is. He's Amitabha Buddha come again. Go bow to him. Leave us alone."

As the official stood there in amazement, the two grimy monks took one last step backwards and disappeared into the rock cliff. That place is now known as Moonlight Cliff on Tian Tai mountain – the spot where Han Shan and Shi De disappeared.

The official hurried back into Guo Qing monastery to bow to the Abbot Feng Kan – Amitabha Buddha. But when he arrived inside, he found that the abbot had sat down and entered the stillness. He had entered nirvana. The official now knew that the abbot had been Amitabha Buddha come again, but it was too late. He had failed to see what was right before his eyes. Amitabha Buddha was already gone.

Why don't Buddhas and Bodhisattvas let people know who they are when they come? If everyone knew, everyone would be bowing all day long one after another to the point that it would be pretty annoying. There would be no time left to cultivate. So they don't want to let on who they are.

That's the way it is in Buddhism. One would never say, "Look! I'm enlightened!" "I'm a Buddha!" People like that are no different from the ones being discussed in this section of the sutra. I've never met anyone who admitted he was enlightened. Neither Elder Master Hsü Yün, nor any of the other enlightened monks in China ever said a word about being enlightened, even if asked directly. There's no such thing in Buddhism, except perhaps in "New Buddhism."

The beings discussed here claim to be superior people. "Do you know who I am? I'm Maitreya Bodhisattva." "Do you know who I am? I'm Guan Shi Yin Bodhisattva. Now that you know, you should not miss out on this opportunity. Bow to me as your teacher. If you don't want to bow to me, you can bow to my teacher. I'll give you a certificate and for sixty-five dollars I'll transmit a teaching to you." They go about **enticing and deceiving the ignorant.** They confuse unsuspecting people. I've met so many people like this.

Their line is, "I have special methods. I'll sell you one for only three hundred dollars. It's only because I like you so much that I've saved it for you. If I were not fond of you, I wouldn't offer it to you."

So the disciple gives the teacher three hundred dollars in exchange for a treasure. Some hit you up for a thousand dollars. Soon the old teacher's wallet is fat. When he moves his stash from safe to safe, he has to use a train! Most people fall for this kind of thing. If you speak true dharma for them, such as "Don't kill," they don't believe it. "Don't steal." They don't believe that, either. "Don't be lustful." They don't believe that, either. But if you tell them you've got something that will be to their advantage, they'll pay you for it. **Or frightening them out of their wits**. They make you lose whatever wisdom you had. They make you confused. **They disrupt and lay waste to households wherever they go.** They are really filthy rich, but everywhere they go they keep amassing more wealth, stripping householders of their goods, lock, stock, and barrel.

Sutra:

"I teach the bhikshus to beg for their food in an assigned place, in order to help them renounce greed and accomplish the bodhi way. The bhikshus do not prepare their own food, so that, at the end of this life of transitory existence in the triple realm, they can show themselves to be once-returners who go and do not come back.

Commentary:

I teach the bhikshus to beg for their food in an assigned place, in order to help them renounce greed. When it was time to beg for food, each bhikshu headed in a certain direction and made his rounds in a certain locale. Carrying their bowls, the bhikshus went out to receive alms. Why did the Buddha teach them to beg for food? First, when laypeople give food to people who have left the home-life, they can ensure the reward of blessings and put an end to their suffering and distress. Second, when bhikshus go out for alms, they eat whatever they are given. If it's good, they eat it; if it's bad, they eat it just the same. In this way, they get rid of their greed. If you cook for yourself, you'll think, "What I made today wasn't so good; tomorrow, though, I'll make something delicious. The day after that I'll make something even better, and the day after that I'll make something simply spectacular." There's no end to it. When one goes out begging, there is no chance for selection. One does not make distinctions about which food and drink is good and which is not. One cannot say, "The food I've gotten today is really tasty," and then eat with great gusto. And then the next day, if the food one gets is not good, one does not even eat it. That kind of conduct is impermissible. One eats the good and the bad; general idea is to eat one's fill and forget about it. That gets rid of greed.

In this way they can **accomplish the bodhi way**. That is because, as it's said:

> The superior person is concerned about the Way,
>   not about food.

People who come to investigate the Buddhadharma should not get hung up on food.

The bhikshus do not prepare their own food, so that, at the end of this life of transitory existence in the triple realm, they can show themselves to be once-returners who go and do not come back. They only want to eat enough to sustain their bodies. Our life in this world, whether we dwell on land or in water, is like a stay in a hotel – transitory and soon over. Don't be attached to it. The bhikshus put an end to greed, so that when this life in the triple realm is over, they won't have to come back. "This place is filthy. I'm not going to return here," is their thought. Even America, with its beautiful toilets and magnificent houses – it's enough to have been here once. Don't come back! Don't be greedy for toilets. To begin with, they smell bad; why would you be greedy for them? In fact, this whole world stinks. You should not think it is a clean place. This world is a toilet in itself.

Sutra:

"How can thieves put on my robes and sell the Thus Come One, saying that all manner of karma one creates is just the Buddhadharma? They slander those who have left the home-life and regard bhikshus who have taken complete precepts as belonging to the path of the small vehicle. Because of such doubts and misjudgments, limitless living beings fall into the Relentless Hell.

Commentary:

How can thieves put on my robes? They don the clothes of a left-home person and tell people, "I am a dharma master who can lecture on the sutras. You should all believe in me." **And** they **sell the Thus Come One.** They barter with the Buddhadharma. They do business with it. All they do is think of ways to get people to give them money. They say **that all manner of karma one creates is just the Buddhadharma.** They say, "Everything is the Buddhadharma. Dancing is Buddhadharma; drinking wine is Buddhadharma; making music is Buddhadharma. These are all part of the Buddha's eighty-four thousand dharma-doors." They are really smooth talkers. "Smoking cigarettes is Buddhadharma, gambling is Buddhadharma; you can do anything you want." They are lax, even to the point that no matter what one might do, they say it's all right. **They slander those who have left the home-life and regard bhikshus who have taken complete precepts as belonging to the path of the small vehicle.** If anyone calls them on it and asks, "Have you taken the complete precepts?" they don't even know what you are talking about. They don't even understand the five precepts, how much the less the eight, or the ten, or the ten major and forty-eight minor precepts. They themselves are not authentic left-home people. Their scope is very small and self-centered. **Because of such doubts and misjudgments limitless living beings fall into the Relentless Hell.** They cause others to be confused, and they themselves basically do not understand. To begin with, the people who follow them had good intentions, but having become involved with such a messed-up teacher, they end up in the same situation as was mentioned earlier:

> If one who is dazed
> transmits the delusion to another,
> When all is said and done,
> neither one understands.
> The teacher falls into the hells,
> And the disciples burrow in after him.

In the Relentless Hell there is no break in the suffering. One person fills the hell in the same way that many people fill it. With just one person in that hell, there would still be no space left over. And no matter how many people are in it, it's always just as full. One can never get out of this hell. So it's very dangerous to set up conditions for it.

Q2 Teaching people to cut off stealing is the Buddha's instruction.
R1 First he offers his own instructions.

Sutra:

"I say that bhikshus who after my extinction have decisive resolve to cultivate samadhi, and who before the images of Thus Come Ones can burn a candle on their bodies, or burn off a finger, or burn even one incense stick on their bodies, will, in that moment, repay their debts from beginningless time past. They can depart from the world and forever be free of outflows. Though they may not have instantly understood the unsurpassed enlightenment, they will already have firmly set their mind on it.

Commentary:

I say that bhikshus who after my extinction have decisive resolve to cultivate samadhi, and who before the images of Thus Come Ones can burn a candle on their bodies, or burn off a finger, or burn even one incense stick on their bodies, will, in that moment, repay their debts from beginningless time past. These bhikshus, under proper guidance, at the appropriate time, and in the prescribed manner, cut out a piece of their flesh with a knife and place some oil in the hole. Then they light the oil and are a living lamp for the Buddha. Or perhaps they burn off a finger in the correct manner; or they let one or two or three pieces of incense burn on their bodies, such as on their arm. Shakyamuni Buddha says that all the debts such people have accumulated throughout time without beginning can be wiped away in that single act. **They can depart from the world and forever be free of outflows. Though they may not have instantly understood the unsurpassed enlightenment, they will already have firmly set their mind on it.** They will have a decisive resolve and will not retreat from it.

Sutra:

"**If one does not practice any of these token renunciations of the body on the causal level, then even if one realizes the unconditioned, one will still have to come back as a person to repay one's past debts exactly as I had to undergo the retribution of having to eat the grain meant for horses.**

Commentary:

"**If one does not practice any of these token renunciations of the body on the causal level, then even if one realizes the unconditioned, one will still have to come back as a person to repay one's past debts.** If one doesn't do any of these acts of physical renunciation, such as making a lamp on one's body or burning off a finger or making incense burns on the body, thus planting a few good causes, then even if one accomplishes the Way, even if one becomes enlightened, even if one becomes a Buddha, one will still have debts to pay back. One will have to come back as a person again and repay one's debts from past lives, **exactly as I had to undergo the retribution of having to eat the grain meant for horses.** I had to eat grain meant for horse-feed for ninety days this life," Shakyamuni Buddha says.

Why did Shakyamuni Buddha have to undergo that retribution? It had to do with a past life, when he was a brahman engaged in teaching five hundred pure youths how to cultivate the Way. At that time, there was another Buddha in the world. One day, when that Buddha went on the begging rounds with the bhikshus, he instructed them to have the donors put a little extra in their bowls to accommodate a bhikshu who was sick and could not go on the alms-rounds. As they returned from their rounds, they passed by the mountain where the brahman who was Shakyamuni Buddha on the cause-ground dwelt. When the brahman got a whiff of the food from their especially full bowls, he became jealous. "Why do those bald monks get to eat so well? They should only be allowed horse-feed." His five-hundred disciples all agreed with him, of course, chiming in, "Right! They are only fit to eat horse-feed." After he became a Buddha, Shakyamuni took five hundred disciples to a certain country to spend the summer retreat. On the surface, the king of the country gave them a cordial welcome, but after he allowed them into the country, the king would not make offerings to these monks. Eventually a horse-trainer in the country became aware that the Buddha and bhikshus were not being given any offerings of food, so he shared with the monks the grain that he fed his horses. Even though the brahman had eventually become Shakyamuni Buddha, and his five hundred pure youths were now five hundred arhats and had been certified to the fruition, they still had to repay the debt from that past life: for ninety days they had to eat horse-feed.

So, the Buddha says that if one does not perform these acts of bodily renunciation, one will still in the future have to repay the debts one has incurred in past lives, just as he did.

R2 Then he explains it is the teaching of all former Buddhas.

Sutra:

"When you teach people in the world to cultivate samadhi, they must also cease stealing. This is the third clear and unalterable instruction on purity given by the Thus Come One and the Buddhas of the past, World Honored Ones.

Commentary:

When you teach people in the world to cultivate samadhi, they must also cease stealing. Since they want to cultivate, they must get rid of their thoughts of stealing. **This is the third clear and unalterable instruction on purity given by the Thus Come One and the Buddhas of the past, World Honored Ones.** This is an unchanging instruction given by Shakyamuni Buddha and by all Buddhas of the past.

P3 He decides if samadhi can be obtained.
Q1 An analogy makes clear that if stealing is not cut off, samadhi is hard to obtain.

Sutra:

"**Therefore, Ananda, if cultivators of Chan samadhi do not cease stealing, they are like someone who pours water into a leaking cup and hopes to fill it. He may continue for as many aeons as there are fine motes of dust, but it still will not be full in the end.**

Commentary:

Therefore, Ananda, if cultivators of Chan samadhi do not cease stealing, they are like someone who pours water into a leaking cup and hopes to fill it. If you are trying to fill a cup with a hole in it, you **may continue for as many aeons as there are fine motes of dust, but it still will not be full in the end.**

Q2 Diligent and profound cutting off of stealing can bring samadhi.

Sutra:

"**If bhikshus do not store away anything but their robes and bowls; if they give what is left over from their food-offerings to hungry living beings; if they put their palms together and make obeisance to the entire great assembly; if when people scold them they can treat it as praise; if they can sacrifice their very bodies and minds, giving their flesh, bones, and blood to living creatures; and if they do not repeat the non-ultimate teachings of the Thus Come One as though they were their own explanations, misrepresenting them to those who have just begun to** study, then the Buddha gives them his seal as having attained true samadhi.

Commentary:

If bhikshus do not store away anything but their robes and bowls. Bhikshus should have three robes, a bowl, and sitting cloth. They don't need anything else. They do not accumulate possessions. **If they give what is left over from their food-offerings to hungry living beings.** They give alms that they cannot eat to living beings who have nothing to eat. **If they put their palms together and make obeisance to the entire great assembly.** They place their palms together and are respectful to any gathering of people. **If when people scold them they can treat it as praise.** Regard scolding as being the same as praise, they do not react to the scolding. **If they can sacrifice their very bodies and minds, giving their flesh, bones, and blood to living creatures.** Their minds harbor no arrogant thoughts and their bodies do not act in ways that display pride and self-satisfaction. When someone scolds you, you should act as if he is singing a song for you. If you yourself do not scold people and yet someone scolds you, you shouldn't even understand what he is saying. It shouldn't even make sense to you. It should be as if he is speaking some language you don't understand, such as Japanese, English, or Chinese, depending on which one you don't know. When someone is clearly scolding you, you just think, "Oh, he is saying such nice things about me." Look at it in the reverse. If someone hits you, just pretend you bumped into a wall. Suppose you were careless and ran smack into a wall and were left with a big lump on your head. If you then turned around and socked the wall with your fist, saying, "Why did bump into me?" you'd only end up with a hurt hand to boot. When someone strikes you, if you view it as if you had bumped into a wall, the whole affair will end right there.

True bhikshus who have brought forth the resolve for bodhi should even give up their flesh and blood to other beings if there are some who want to partake of it. Once when Shakyamuni Buddha was on the cause-ground, he saw a starving tiger, and he gave up his body for the tiger to eat. The tiger is one of the world's most ferocious beasts, and yet the Buddha on the cause-ground could give up his own body to the tiger.

If they do not repeat the non-ultimate teachings of the Thus Come One as though they were their own explanations, misrepresenting them to those who have just begun to study. They will not discuss the teachings of the small vehicle in such a way that they appear to be their own explanations. In other words, they won't plagiarize the Buddha, thereby misrepresenting themselves and confusing people who have first begun to study. If they do not do any of these things, **then the Buddha gives them his seal as having attained true samadhi.** The Buddha will give the seal of certification to people like this. They have genuine samadhi power.

Sutra:

"What I have said here is the Buddhas' teaching. Any explanation counter to it is the teaching of Papiyan.

Commentary:

This explanation is the way the Buddhas speak dharma. Any other explanation is the instructions given by the kings of demons.

One Must Cut Off False Speech

N4 One must cut off false speech.
O1 He discusses the intent of precepts or provisional teachings.
P1 False speech is very harmful.
Q1 Traces false speech as a reason for becoming demonic.

Sutra:

"**Ananda, though living beings in the six paths of any mundane world may not kill, steal, or lust either physically or mentally, these three aspects of their conduct thus being perfect. Yet if they tell lies, the samadhi they attain will not be pure. They will become demons of love and views and will lose the seed of the Thus Come One.**

Commentary:

Ananda, though living beings in the six paths of any mundane world may not kill, steal, or lust either physically or mentally. With their bodies they do not commit acts of killing, stealing, or lust. In their minds there are no thoughts of killing, stealing, or lust, **these three aspects of their conduct thus being perfect, yet if they tell lies, the samadhi they attain will not be pure.** This means it is a habit with them: they are always telling big lies. Since they are not pure, **they will become demons of love and views and will lose the seed of the Thus Come One.** They will become demons of love or demons of views. Why do they lose the seed of the Tathagata? It is because they lie excessively.

Q2 Points out the motives of false speech.

Sutra:

"**They say that they have attained what they have not attained, and that they have been certified when they have not been certified. Perhaps they seek to be foremost in the world, the most venerated and superior person. To their audiences they say that they have attained the fruition of a shrotaapanna, the fruition of a sakridagamin, the fruition of an anagamin, the fruition of arhatship, the pratyekabuddha vehicle, or the various levels of bodhisattvahood up to and including the ten grounds, in order to be revered by others and because they are greedy for offerings.**

Commentary:

What kind of lies do they tell? Ordinary lies aside, **they say that they have attained what they have not attained.** They have not attained the Way. Basically, they don't understand the least thing about cultivating. They don't know how to recite the Buddha's name; they don't know how to hold precepts; they don't know how to sit in Chan. They act like they know, but they don't. They hear someone explain some principle, and they interrupt with, "I understand that. I already knew that a long time ago." Or they say, "Hey, I've already got the Way. I'm enlightened. I'm a Buddha." They say **that they have been certified when they have not been certified.** They have not reached the first stage of arhatship, much less do they have an understanding of the levels above that, but they say, "Do you know what I am? I'm an arhat." Or, "I'm a Buddha." Or, "I'm a bodhisattva." Why do they say these things? **Perhaps they seek to be foremost in the world, the most venerated and superior person.** It's as someone said recently to one of my disciples: "What sect are you? We're in this together. We should join ranks, and I'll be the leader. I'm the founder of American Buddhism. I'm the first patriarch of American Buddhism." That's "seeking to be number one." **To their audiences they say that they have attained the fruition of a shrotaapanna, the fruition of a** sakridagamin, the fruition of an anagamin, the fruition of arhatship. They start out telling those around them that they are first-stage arhats. But soon that level is not lofty enough, so they say, "Oh, I just certified to the second fruition of arhatship!" And then a second later they claim fruition to the fourth level. Still, fourth fruition is just arhatship and not the highest position, so they are not satisfied. They claim to have **the pratyekabuddha vehicle, of the various levels of bodhisattvahood up to and including the ten grounds.** They start telling people they are pratyekabuddhas, or they claim to be at any one of the stages of bodhisattva practice, even the ten grounds!

Why do such people claim to be arhats, pratyekabuddhas, and bodhisattvas? What it amounts to is that they are cheating people and telling big lies in order to get people to believe in them. If no one believes in them, they don't have an income. As soon as people believe, then the offerings start to pour in. And so intent are they **to be revered by others,** so **greedy** are they **for their offerings,** that they do not fear falling into the Hell of Pulling Out Tongues. If one is a liar, after one's death, one goes to this hell where an iron hook sinks into one's tongue, pulls it out, and a sword chops it off. That's the retribution for lying. And yet there are still people who dare to do it. We don't even have to look beyond this world: just take mutes, for instance. Why are they mute? They are undergoing a retribution for excessive lying. They get to be people, but they can't talk. "See how much lying you can do now!" is the message. Why can't they talk? They have had their tongues cut out. Although they have tongues, the essence in them is gone; their tongues have no nature.

Why are some people blind? It is because they looked down on other people. They always considered themselves to be better than everyone else. They were smarter and more talented in every way, and so in this life they can't see people. Now they must ask themselves whether they are really better than everyone else. The deaf also are undergoing a retribution for having eavesdropped on conversations. They used to put their ear to numerous keyholes to find out what was being said. Present-day spies with their myriad ways of overhearing people, of stealing private conversations, may well have to bear the same retribution and be deaf at some future point in time.

However, if once you understand the principle, you then refrain from lying, you can avoid being mute. If you no longer look down on people, you won't have to be blind. If you don't steal other's conversations, you won't have to be deaf. Being mute, hunchback, and blind are all retributions for having slandered the Triple Jewel.

Q3 Predicts the fall of those who harm the good.

Sutra:

"These icchantikas destroy the seeds of Buddhahood just as surely as a tala tree is destroyed if it is chopped down. The Buddha predicts that such people sever their good roots forever and lose their knowledge and vision. Immersed in the sea of the three sufferings, they cannot attain samadhi.

Commentary:

These icchantikas destroy the seeds of Buddhahood. People who tell big lies, who say they have attained what they in fact have not attained, who say they have been certified to what they have not been certified to, and who say they understand things they do not understand – such people are "icchantikas," which means "those who have cut off their good roots." If you cut off your good roots, then of course your bad roots will multiply. People who tell big lies and cheat people in the world ruin their own Buddha seed, **just as surely as a tala tree is destroyed if it is chopped down.** The tala tree, found in India, grows to great heights, but if it is chopped down, it will not grow again. These people sever their Buddha seed in the same way one might cut down a tala tree; neither will grow again. **The Buddha predicts that such people sever their good roots forever and lose their knowledge and vision.** The Buddha's prediction for such people is that they ruin their own good roots and become bereft of any sense or insight. **Immersed in the sea of the**

three sufferings, they cannot attain samadhi. The three sufferings referred to here are:

1. The suffering of knives, which refers to the hell of the mountain of knives;
2. The suffering of blood, which refers to the hell of bleeding, where one's entire body keeps bleeding and bleeding;
3. The suffering of fire, which refers to the hell of burning by fire.

These people fall into these three terrible hells.

P2　He shows that he has clearly instructed against false speech.
Q1　The Buddha instructs that holy transformations must be secret.

Sutra:

"**I command the bodhisattvas and arhats to appear after my extinction in response-bodies in the Dharma-ending Age, and to take various forms in order to rescue those in the cycle of rebirth.**

Commentary:

I command the bodhisattvas and arhats to appear after my extinction in response-bodies in the Dharma-ending Age. They should use response bodies and transformation bodies to be born in this world where there is so much suffering and distress. During the Dharma-ending Age, they will take various forms, they will appear in various ways – perhaps as human beings, perhaps as animals, or in any one of a manner of forms. They will constantly accord with living beings **in order to rescue those in the cycle of rebirth.** They will universally save living beings. Bodhisattvas come back as animals as well. You shouldn't think that it is disrespectful to say so, because they really do. In their practice of the bodhisattva way, they will go and teach animals, as when Shakyamuni Buddha in a past life was a deer king and rescued the deer.

Sutra:

"They should either become shramanas, white-robed laypeople, kings, ministers or officials, virgin youths or maidens, and so forth, even prostitutes, widows, profligates, thieves, butchers, or dealers in contraband, doing the same things as these kinds of people while they praise the Buddha vehicle and cause them to enter samadhi in body and mind.

Commentary:

These bodhisattvas and arhats make transformation bodies and **become shramanas**, people who have left the homelife, either fully ordained or novices. Or they become **white-robed laypeople**. Laypeople do not leave the homelife, and they were referred to as "the white-robed" in India. They protect and uphold the Triple Jewel. This is because left-home people

> Do not plow, but must eat,
> Do not sew, but must wear clothes.

So it is necessary for the laypeople to make offerings to them. Or the bodhisattvas become **kings** in the human realm, or **ministers or officials**. Or they become **virgin youths or maidens, and so forth, even prostitutes, widows**. Or they become **profligates, thieves, butchers, or dealers in contraband**. They even become people who force themselves on women, or who steal things, or kill animals, or deal in things like opium. The bodhisattvas and arhats do **the same things as these kinds of people.** Why do they turn into people like those? It is because they want to convert those kinds of people. In order to do this, they must use the four methods to gather people in:

1. giving;
2. kind words;
3. beneficial practice;
4. similar work.

First, they attract them by giving. There are three kinds of giving:

1. the giving of wealth;
2. the giving of dharma;
3. the giving of fearlessness.

If one has money, one gives it. If one knows the dharma, one speaks it for others, thereby giving. If someone is frightened or upset, one can protect them and comfort them, thereby dispelling their fears; that is the giving of fearlessness. But, in giving in these various ways, one should not be greedy and expect repayment of some kind. You should not think, "Ah, now I am giving in this way, and in the future I will gain various advantages." Do it and forget it. Let it go. Then "the substance of the three aspects is empty." The three aspects are the giver, the gift, and the receiver. You should practice giving with the attitude that it is something you should do, rather than that you are amassing all kinds of merit and virtue.

The giving of dharma is the same way. When you speak dharma for others, you should not be thinking, "My merit and virtue from speaking the dharma is no doubt tremendous: you should all make offerings to me." The same is true of the giving of fearlessness. In general, when you give, you should not be reflecting upon how much benefit there is in it for you. Nor should you only be willing to give when you think it will be advantageous for you, while refusing to give when it won't.

Second, they attract them with kind words. For instance, the Buddha says to Ananda, "Good indeed, good indeed," and in the same way the bodhisattvas praise beings, saying, "You are really a good boy! You are so intelligent! You really have good roots."

Third, they attract them with beneficial practices. This means doing things to help others, not to help yourself.

Fourth, they attract them through similar work. That is, whatever beings do, they do. Perhaps a bodhisattva wants to save a prostitute who has good roots that have come to maturity; Matangi's daughter, mentioned in this sutra, is an example. Matangi's daughter was a prostitute, but her time was right, and so when Ananda returned to the Jeta Grove, she followed along. As soon as the Buddha spoke dharma for her, she was certified as having attained the third fruition of arhatship. Eventually she attained the fourth fruition. And she was a prostitute to start with! So, in order to save prostitutes, bodhisattvas may transform into prostitutes themselves, because if they are engaged in the same profession and are friends, what they say will be trusted by those they wish to save. For instance, a university student may say, "I believe in the Buddhadharma; it's wonderful. I'm going to investigate such and such a sutra right now." The students he is talking to say, "We'd like to go, too. We'd also like to look into that sutra." So everyone comes to investigate the *Shurangama Sutra*. It's the same principle.

Therefore, you never know who might be a bodhisattva or an arhat. But, if you are one, don't tell anyone. You don't want to go around saying, "I'm a bodhisattva. You should listen to what I have to say." Why can't you do that? Because the Buddha forbade it.

So the bodhisattvas and arhats do the same things as these kinds of people, but while doing it **they praise the Buddha vehicle and cause them to enter samadhi in body and mind.** They may indulge in the same activities, but they speak the Buddhadharma at every chance they get. "The Buddhadharma is so fine! It's beyond compare." And in this way, they cause those who listen to be enticed, just as if they were eating candy.

That reminds me of an historical record. In the past, in China, there lived a monk named Du Xun. He would sometimes lecture sutras and speak dharma. He also taught people how to sit and investigate Chan. Sometimes he taught people to be mindful of the Buddha. He used all kinds of methods to teach and transform living beings. He had a disciple who left the home-life under him and followed him for more than ten years. Every day, the disciple was very attentive to the teacher's conduct and activities. He kept trying to figure out what his teacher was: that is, was he a bodhisattva, or an arhat, or perhaps a Buddha? Finally, after ten years, he came to the conclusion that his teacher, Dharma Master Du Xun, was absolutely ordinary, that there was nothing unusual about him. The teacher ate, as did other people. The teacher wore clothes, as did other people. The teacher slept, as did other people. He wasn't any different from anyone else. So the disciple decided he probably wasn't a Buddha or a bodhisattva, or an arhat. With that, he went to his teacher to bow out. He decided to leave. What were his plans? He was going to Wu Tai mountain to bow to Manjushri Bodhisattva. He intended to seek wisdom from Manjushri Bodhisattva with the hope of becoming enlightened. "Teacher," he said, "I've studied here for more than ten years, and I don't feel I've learned anything. I don't understand anything, and I'm really stupid, so I've decided to go bow to Manjushri Bodhisattva in the hope that I can realize some wisdom."

"Fine," said his teacher. "You want to go climb that mountain, so be it. Be on your way. But I have two letters I'd like you to take along for me and deliver on your way." One letter was for Old Mother Pig. The other letter was for Madam Green. When the disciple reached the address that was written on Madam Green's letter, she turned out to be a prostitute. The disciple was getting suspicious. "What's my teacher doing writing letters to a prostitute?" he wondered. "Is she his lover, and he's having me be the go-between?" But he delivered the letter saying, "My teacher, Du Xun, sent you a letter." Madam Green took the letter, read it, sat down, and said, "Good! He's leaving. I'm leaving, too." Then she died on the spot. She entered nirvana. The disciple found the whole event quite strange, and so he took the letter and read it. Then he found out that Madam Green was really Guan Shi Yin Bodhisattva, for the letter said, "Guan Yin, I've finished my business here and am going. You should come with me."

The disciple sighed with regret. "If I had known that was Guan Yin Bodhisattva, I would have knelt before her, and until she had entered nirvana I would have never gotten up, so I could have sought for wisdom and enlightenment. That would have been great, but now I've missed the opportunity." That's just exactly what's meant by the saying:

Face to face with her,
one fails to recognize Guan Shi Yin.

He took up the other letter and headed for Old Mother Pig's place. But when he got to the address, no one had heard of her. As he was passing a pigsty, an old sow spoke to him. "Why are you looking for Old Mother Pig?"

The disciple was astonished and wondered what kind of freak he had encountered. Impulsively he replied, "My teacher told me to deliver a letter to Old Mother Pig."

"Oh," said the sow. "Well, I'm Old Mother Pig. You can give me the letter." The sow took the letter and looked at it, though it was hard to know whether she could understand what it said. Nonetheless, when she finished looking at it, she sat down and said, "Oh, his business is finished; I'll go back, too," and she died.

When the disciple looked at the letter, it showed the old pig was a transformation body of Universal Worthy Bodhisattva. "Is it really possible that Universal Worthy was that pig?" he wondered, still plagued with doubts. And he didn't have any idea what business it was that his teacher had finished.

He went on to Wu Tai mountain, and there he saw a very old monk, who asked him, "What are you doing here?"

"I came to bow to the greatly wise Manjushri Bodhisattva and to seek for wisdom and enlightenment."

"Ugh, you!" said the old monk. "You've come to bow to Manjushri Bodhisattva, but bowing to your own teacher is ten thousand times better."

"Why?" asked the disciple.

"Your teacher, the Venerable Du Xun, is Amitabha Buddha appearing in the world again. He's come to roam and play in the human realm to teach and transform living beings. You've been his disciple for more than ten years. How come you've never figured that out?"

"Oh? My teacher is Amitabha Buddha!" said the disciple. "He doesn't look like him!" And when he looked again, the old monk was gone. Then he saw a note there which said, "Manjushri Bodhisattva instructs you to immediately return to your teacher Du Xun, who is Amitabha Buddha."

Finally, the disciple believed it. He had met Manjushri Bodhisattva in the flesh and been told to go back to his own teacher. So he rushed back only to find that the monk, Du Xun, had entered the stillness days before. Once again, he had missed his chance. He had been the disciple of Amitabha Buddha for a decade and never realized it. He renounced what was at hand to seek what was afar, only to find that he should return to his own teacher. Now who was there left to see?

Sutra:

"But they should never say of themselves, 'I am truly a bodhisattva'; or 'I am truly an arhat,' or let the Buddha's secret cause leak out by speaking casually to those who have not yet studied.

Commentary:

But they should never say of themselves, "I am truly a bodhisattva." They might be bodhisattvas, arhats, or Buddhas who have come to this world. But even if it were Shakyamuni Buddha himself come again to this world, or Amitabha Buddha, or Medicine Master Buddha Who Dispels Calamities and Lengthens Life, or Production of Jewels Buddha, or Accomplishment Buddha, or any other Buddha, or any bodhisattva or arhat, not one would ever say, "I'm really a bodhisattva. It's true, and you should believe me. I'm truly a bodhisattva!" One cannot speak like that.

If they say, **"I am truly an arhat.** Do you recognize me? Do you realize who I am? I'm an arhat!" then you know they are part of the retinue of the demon kings. If someone praises you by saying that you are a bodhisattva or an arhat, you should not admit it even if you are. You cannot let it out. You cannot **let the Buddha's secret cause leak out.** You should not reveal the secret cause of the

Buddha **by speaking casually to those who have not yet studied.** You can't just nonchalantly reveal your origin. What is acceptable, then? You can reveal it when you are about to die; don't do it before you are ready to go.

> When you reveal it,
> then don't stay.
> As long as you are staying,
> don't reveal it.

As soon as you reveal your origins, for example, that you are a transformation body of such and such a bodhisattva, then you should leave immediately. As long as the word is not out, you can stay here, but as soon as you let it be known, you'll wind up with a lot of trouble on your hands if you don't go.

Q2 Only at the end of their life is there a transmission.

Sutra:

"How can people who make such claims, other than at the end of their lives and then only to those who inherit the teaching, be doing anything but deluding and confusing living beings and indulging in a gross false claim?

Commentary:

How can people who make such claims, other than at the end of their lives and then only to those who inherit the teaching, be doing anything but deluding and confusing living beings? If you are a holy being, then at the end of your life you can tell people so. But even then you can't tell everyone. You reveal it to those closest to you, perhaps a room-entering disciple or two. People who do otherwise simply delude and confuse beings by **indulging in a gross false claim.** If you have not attained the Way, and you claim you have, if you have not been certified to the fruition, and you say that you have, you are telling a huge lie.

During the Qing dynasty in China lived the high monk Elder Master Yin Guang. The master was from Shan Xi. After he left the home-life, he made a pilgrimage to Pu Tou mountain, the bodhimanda of Guan Shi Yin Bodhisattva. He went into seclusion there. He locked himself in a room and read the Tripitaka. If one reads every day, it takes about three years to finish reading the Tripitaka. He repeated this three-year cycle of reading the Tripitaka over and over for eighteen years. During all those years, he never left the mountain. At the end of that period, a group of laypeople in Shanghai invited him to lecture on the *Amitabha Sutra*. He agreed, but not too many people came to the lecture series, perhaps because it was difficult for them to understand his Shanghai dialect.

But among those who did come was a high school student from Shanghai who had had a dream in which she was told to go listen to the sutra. The dream said: "You should go to such and such a lay community and listen to the *Amitabha Sutra* being lectured there by Great Strength Bodhisattva." The next night, the student read in the newspaper that Dharma Master Yin Guang was lecturing the *Amitabha Sutra* at that very place. "Why did my dream tell me that Dharma Master Yin Guang is Great Strength Bodhisattva?" she wondered.

That night, she attended the lecture, and after everyone had left she related her dream to the elder dharma master. When she concluded that he must be Great Strength Bodhisattva, Dharma Master Yin Guang was very displeased, and he warned her, "You cannot go around talking such nonsense!" So she never talked about the dream, but she took refuge with the elder dharma master. Three years later the master entered the stillness, and it was only then that she spoke about her dream. Everyone was upset that she had not told them sooner, so that they could have requested more dharma from the elder master. But she told them she had been forbidden to speak of it by the master himself. From this incident it is clear that Elder Master Yin Guang was, in fact, a transformation of Great Strength Bodhisattva. When he was cremated, there were many sharira.

So, when one's life is about to end, some hints can be given. But still, one can't speak openly about such things. Perhaps in a dream, as in this case, a little indication can be made. But one cannot state anything flatly like, "I am Great Strength Bodhisattva." That's not the way it's done.

People these days go around claiming to be Buddhas. This is in direct opposition to the teachings of the *Shurangama Sutra*. Of course, all living beings are Buddhas, but you have to cultivate to become a Buddha. If you don't cultivate, you're more likely to become a horse, cow, pig, sheep, or chicken. You're likely to become a hungry ghost or fall into the hells; nothing is for certain.

P3 The clear instruction transmitted from former Buddhas.

Sutra:

"**When you teach people in the world to cultivate samadhi, they must also cease all lying. This is the fourth clear and unalterable instruction on purity given by the Thus Come Ones and the Buddhas of the past, World Honored Ones.**

Commentary:

Ananda, do you hear this? **When you teach people in the world to cultivate samadhi, they must also cease all lying.** This means all kinds of exaggerations and boasts. For goodness sake, don't say, "I'm enlightened," or "I've been certified to the fruition," or "I'm a Buddha," or "I'm a bodhisattva," or "I'm an arhat." That's just too cheap. **This is the fourth clear and unalterable instruction on purity given by the Thus Come Ones and the Buddhas of the past, World Honored Ones.** Don't teach others to lie and make false claims. This instruction is given by all Buddhas of the present and all Buddhas of the past.

P4 Deciding if bodhi can be obtained.
Q1 An analogy shows that if one does not cut off false speech, it is difficult to obtain bodhi.

Sutra:

"**Therefore, Ananda, one who does not cut off lying is like a person who carves a piece of human excrement to look like** chandana, hoping to make it fragrant. **He is attempting the impossible.**

Commentary:

I'll give you an example. **Therefore, Ananda,** you should realize that **one who does not cut off lying is like a person who carves a piece of human excrement to look like chandana, hoping to make it fragrant.** Someone who hopes to become pure without cutting off lying is like a person who tries to make a piece of incense out of a piece of shit. **He is attempting the impossible.** He'll never get the excrement to smell like chandana incense. This means if you lie, it's as if you smell bad. If you cultivate Chan samadhi trying to become a Buddha and yet you continue to lie, you are just like a piece of excrement. For a liar to try and become a Buddha is like trying to get a piece of shit to be a sweet-smelling Buddha image. That's beyond reason.

Sutra:

"I teach the bhikshus that the straight mind is the bodhimanda and that they should practice the four awesome deportments in all their activities. Since they should be devoid of all falseness, how can they claim to have themselves attained the abilities of a superior person?

Commentary:

I teach the bhikshus that the straight mind is the bodhimanda. Here the reference to "bhikshus" includes all four assemblies. You can't say at this point, "I'm a layperson, and so the Buddha isn't referring to me." You have to be straight in what you think and say. Don't be roundabout. Don't be deceptive. Not having a straight mind is also like trying to get incense out of excrement.

I tell them **that they should practice the four awesome deportments in all their activities.** These were discussed in detail earlier. There are 250 aspects to each of the deportments of standing, sitting, walking, and lying down. You should always do things truly, and actually cultivate. **Since they should be devoid of all falseness, how can they claim to have themselves attained the** abilities of a superior person? How can one say of oneself that one has been certified to the fruition of a bodhisattva or of an arhat? One may not speak that way. Before one has heard the sutras, one may be quite casual in what one says. But, now that you have heard this sutra, you know that you cannot say you have attained certain levels of fruition. To do so is to speak a great lie. The retribution for it is to fall into the Hell of Pulling Out Tongues. In the future, your tongue will be hooked with an iron hook and pulled out by the root. Afterwards you will have no opportunity to lie, for in the future, you will be mute.

Sutra:

"That would be like a poor person falsely calling himself an emperor; for that, he would be taken and executed. Much less should one attempt to usurp the title of Dharma King. When the cause-ground is not true, the effects will be distorted. One who seeks the Buddha's bodhi in this way is like a person who tries to bite his own navel. Who could possibly succeed?

Commentary:

That would be like a poor person falsely calling himself an emperor. "Did you realize," he would say, "that I am the ruler of this land?" **For** saying **that, he would be taken and executed.** The emperor would immediately have him arrested, and his whole family would be wiped out. All his friends and relatives would die in the process. Then where would the "emperor" have gone? To claim that you have attained the fruition when you have not is to be like a poor person who calls himself emperor. He'll be exterminated for it. And if one can't casually call oneself emperor on the worldly plane, **much less should one attempt to usurp the title of Dharma King.** How could one try to usurp the position of Buddhahood? **When the cause-ground is not true, the effects will be distorted.** On the cause-ground, when you are cultivating the Way, if you do not cultivate truly, the effects you reap in the future will be crooked. There will be a lot of wrinkles. You will not be able to accomplish the fruition directly. If you cultivate in this way, you may do so for countless great aeons, but you will still be unsuccessful. **One who seeks the Buddha's bodhi in this way is like a person who tries to bite his own navel.** If you conduct yourself in this fashion – continually indulging in lies and boasts and yet are seeking the bodhi of the Buddhas, you are like a person trying to bite his own navel. **Who could possibly succeed?** You could never bite your own navel, because your mouth won't reach it.

Q2 He promises if one can cut off false speech, one will certainly accomplish bodhi.

Sutra:

"**If bhikshus' minds are as straight as lute strings, true and real in everything they do, then they can enter samadhi and never be involved in the deeds of demons. I certify that such people will accomplish the bodhisattvas' unsurpassed knowledge and enlightenment.**

Commentary:

If bhikshus' and laypeoples' **minds are as straight as lute strings, true and real in everything they do, then they can enter samadhi and never be involved in the deeds of demons.** One's mind should be straight like a lute-string, not curved and crooked like the body of the lute. One should be truthful in all matters and never lie. Lying is a case of,

> Being off by a hair in the beginning,
> One will be off by a thousand miles in the end.

If you tell one lie now, it sets back your accomplishment of Buddhahood by several million great aeons. Take a good look and see who's taking the loss.

If one can be straight and truthful, one can enter samadhi, and no demonic obstacles will ever arise. **I certify that such people will accomplish the bodhisattvas' unsurpassed knowledge and enlightenment.** Anyone who has a mind as straight and true as a lute-string can become a bodhisattva. They can accomplish the unsurpassed wisdom and enlightenment of a bodhisattva.

O2 He speaks of the division into deviant and proper.

Sutra:

"What I have said here is the Buddha's teaching. Any explanation counter to it is the teaching of Papiyan.

Commentary:

What I have said here is the Buddha's teaching. If you explain as I have explained here, it will be the doctrine spoken by the Buddhas. **Any explanation counter to it is the teaching of Papiyan.** Anyone who does not express this doctrine, but pronounces theories that oppose it, is just a demon king talking. "Papiyan" refers to the demon king.

M3 General conclusion: stay distant from demons.

Sutra:

"Ananda, you asked about collecting one's thoughts; I have now begun to explain the wonderful method of cultivation for entrance into samadhi. Those who seek the bodhisattva way must first be as pure as glistening frost in keeping these four rules of deportment. If one is able to never give rise to anything superfluous, then the three evils of the mind and the four of the mouth will have no cause to come forth.

Commentary:

Ananda, you asked about collecting one's thoughts; I have now begun to explain the wonderful method of cultivation for entrance into samadhi. The "wonderful method" is the perfect penetration of the organ of the ear, the returning of the hearing to hear the self-nature, so that one's nature accomplishes the Unsurpassed Way. **Those who seek the bodhisattva way must first be as pure as glistening frost in keeping these four rules of deportment.** The first thing you must do is cultivate these four rules of deportment: not taking life, not stealing, not committing acts of sexual misconduct, and not lying. The prohibition against sexual misconduct refers not only to lust with the body, but to lust within the mind. You must get rid of both in order to transcend the wearisome dust. If you don't get rid of your thoughts of lust, you cannot get out of the dust. The same goes for killing, stealing, and lying. These four rules of deportment are extremely important. You should become as glistening white as frost. You should be completely white, without the least bit of defilement – with not one black fleck in the white. If one can be like that, then quite naturally, **one is able to never give rise to anything superfluous.** Spontaneously, you will attain the source. **Then the three evils of the mind and the four of the mouth will have no cause to come forth.** The greed, hatred, and stupidity born of the mind will cease to arise. And the four mistakes of the mouth – loose speech, harsh speech, lies, and gossip will not arise. There will be no causes and conditions to allow them to arise, because you hold the precepts and truly cultivate the four clear and unalterable instructions on purity.

Sutra:

"**Ananda, if one does not neglect these four matters, and, further, if one does not pursue forms, fragrances, tastes, or objects of touch, then how can any demonic deeds arise?**

Commentary:

Ananda, if one does not neglect these four matters, if one does not lose sight of or forget about these four clear and fixed instructions on purity regarding killing, stealing, sexual misconduct, **and, further, if one does not pursue forms, fragrances, tastes, or objects of touch, then how can any demonic deeds arise?** If you don't get caught up in the defiling states of forms, sounds, smells, and objects of touch, if you don't climb on these conditions, then demonic deeds will spontaneously disappear. Once they are gone, they cannot arise.

L2 Aided by the power of the mantra.
M1 Supreme praise for diligently holding it.

Sutra:

"**If there are people who cannot put an end to their habits from the past, you should teach them to single-mindedly recite** my 'light atop the Buddha's summit' unsurpassed spiritual mantra, Mwo He Sa Dan Dwo Bwo Da La.

Commentary:

If there are living beings who cannot get rid of their bad habits from past lives, you should teach them to recite single-mindedly. The important point here is to be single-minded. Don't have a divided mind such that on the one hand you recite the mantra, but on other you doubt its function. You don't want to be reciting and thinking, "Namo, Namo, Namo what?" You recite the mantra on the one hand, and on the other you don't really want to be saying "Namo," at the same time that you are saying it. That's just a case of being caught between belief and doubt. You are basically one person, but you end up with two minds. One mind thinks that perhaps there is some usefulness to the recitation, while the other mind says, "What am I doing reciting things that I don't even understand?" That kind of division is to be feared. You must recite single-mindedly.

"Mwo He" means "great." "Sa Dan Dwo Bwo Da La" refers to the "great white canopy." When you recite "San Dan Dwo Bwo Da La," a great white canopy manifests in the emptiness where you are. The size of the canopy depends on the amount of your skill. If your skill is great and lofty, then when you recite this phrase of the canopy, there will be no disasters for thousands of miles around. If your skill is small, then the canopy will cover your own head and protect you alone. If one has virtue in the Way, if one is a great and virtuous high Sanghan, then when one recites this line of mantra, the entire country can benefit from it. The entire area will be free from calamities; great disasters will turn into small ones, and small disasters won't even happen.

Now we are having the Shurangama-lecture dharma assembly, and a lot of people are cultivating the secret dharma of the Buddha, so I believe that all of America is benefiting from it. Americans may not be aware of it, but we are saving their lives. It is all done invisibly, and they never have any idea of who has saved them or even that they have been saved. Nor do we wish them to know. This is a case of there being no giver and no receiver. The three-wheeled substance of the giver, the gift, and the receiver is empty. When we save people, it is not necessary to get them to thank us. This is where the wonder lies.

Sutra:

"It is the invisible appearance atop the summit of the Thus Come One. It is the spiritual mantra proclaimed by the Buddha of the unconditioned mind who comes forth from the summit in a blaze of light and sits upon a jeweled lotus flower.

Commentary:

The Shurangama Mantra **is the invisible appearance atop the summit of the Thus Come One.** It cannot be seen by people's ordinary physical eyes. As the sutra later describes it,

"At that time, a hundred brilliant rays sprang from the mound of the flesh on the crown of the World Honored One's head. A thousand-petalled precious lotus arose from amidst those rays. Upon the precious flower sat the Thus Come One's transformation.

"From the crown of that Buddha's head, in turn, ten beams of light shone forth, each composed of a hundred rays of precious light. Every one of those glowing rays shone on lands as many as the sands of ten Ganges Rivers, while throughout empty space there were Vajra Secret Traces spirits, each holding aloft a mountain and wielding a pestle.

"The great assembly, gazing upward, felt fearful admiration and sought the Buddha's kind protection. Single-mindedly they listened as the Thus Come One in the light at the invisible appearance on the crown of the Buddha's head proclaimed the spiritual mantra."

I know this passage by heart. I'll never forget it. It is **the Buddha of the unconditioned mind who comes forth from the** summit in a blaze of light and sits upon a jeweled lotus flower, and proclaims the spiritual mantra. People who are able to encounter this spiritual mantra have great good roots from the past. Otherwise, even if they encountered it, they could not learn it. They would never be able to memorize it. That's why I'm testing you on the Shurangama Mantra. Two have already passed the test. The rest of you had better get busy.

M2 He also shows it is not difficult to get rid of these habits.

Sutra:

"What is more, your past lives with Matangi's daughter created accumulated kalpas of causes and conditions. Your habits of fondness and emotional love go back not just one life, nor even just one kalpa. Yet, as soon as I proclaimed it, she was freed forever from the love in her heart and accomplished arhatship."

Commentary:

What is more, your past lives with Matangi's daughter created accumulated kalpas of causes and conditions. Your affinities go way back. You were married to each other five hundred times. **Your habits of fondness and emotional love go back not just one life, nor even just one kalpa.** You two have very deep habits of mutual regard and fondness for each other. It does not pertain to just one time, nor to one life, nor even to just one kalpa. It's been going on for a long, long time. **Yet, as soon as I proclaimed it, she was freed forever from the love in her heart.** Matangi's daughter renounced her emotional love, and she **accomplished arhatship.** After she heard the mantra and returned to receive the Buddha's instruction, she became enlightened and was certified to the third fruition of arhatship. When Manjushri spoke about perfect penetration, she was certified to the fourth fruition of arhatship. Her accomplishment of the fourth fruition was very quick. Ananda is still at the first fruition at this point. He hasn't made any progress.

Sutra:

"**That prostitute, who had no intention of cultivating, was imperceptibly aided by that spiritual power and was swiftly certified to the position beyond learning; then what about you sound-hearers in the assembly, who seek the most supreme vehicle and are resolved to accomplish Buddhahood? For you it should be as easy as tossing dust into a favorable wind. What, then, is the problem?**

Commentary:

That prostitute, who had no intention of cultivating, was imperceptibly aided by that spiritual power and was swiftly certified to the position beyond learning. Matangi's daughter was a prostitute. She basically wasn't interested in cultivating the Way. Nonetheless, the power of the spiritual mantra aided her in a secret way, and she attained the fourth fruition of arhatship very quickly. **Then what about you sound-hearers in the assembly, who seek the most supreme vehicle and are resolved to accomplish Buddhahood?** You sound-hearers in this dharma assembly are in search of the Buddha-vehicle and will certainly become Buddhas. **For you it should be as easy as tossing dust into a favorable wind. What, then, is the problem?** Once a good wind takes the dust, the dust will blow away. What's the difficulty? What's the danger? There isn't any.

K2 A general explanation of samadhi and wisdom in the bodhimanda.
L1 Because of precepts one produces samadhi.

Sutra:

"**Those in the final age who wish to sit in a bodhimanda must first hold the pure precepts of a bhikshu. To do so, they must find as their teacher a foremost shramana who is pure in the precepts. If they do not encounter a member of the Sangha who is truly pure, then it is absolutely certain that their deportment in precepts and rules cannot be accomplished.**

Commentary:

Those in the final age who wish to sit in a bodhimanda must first hold the pure precepts of a bhikshu. The first thing that people in the Dharma-ending Age have to do if they wish to set up bodhimandas – perhaps temples or stupas or Way-places of other sorts – is receive the bhikshu precepts and then uphold them purely. Anyone who wants to leave the home-life must take the precepts in order to do so. Once one has received the precepts, one is a bhikshu. Then one must strictly uphold the precepts and rules. There must not be the slightest violation. **To do so, they must find as their teacher a foremost shramana who is pure in the precepts.** They look for a nationally respected shramana, a high Sanghan. They take him as their teacher. **If they do not encounter a member of the Sangha who is truly pure, then it is absolutely certain that their deportment in precepts and rules cannot be accomplished.** If you don't find a member of the Sangha who holds the precepts purely, then your own deportment with regard to the precepts and rules cannot be brought to fulfillment. You won't be successful in it.

Sutra:

"After accomplishing the precepts, they should put on fresh, clean clothes, light incense in a place where they are alone, and recite the spiritual mantra spoken by the Buddha of the Mind one hundred and eight times. After that, they should secure the boundaries and establish the bodhimanda.

Commentary:

After successfully **accomplishing the precepts, they should put on fresh, clean clothes.** New clothes are best, or clean ones that have not been worn. They should **light incense in a place where they are alone.** You should light incense before the Buddhas and not do anything else but **recite the spiritual mantra spoken by the Buddha of the Mind one hundred and eight times.** "The Buddha of the Mind" refers to the transformation Buddha atop the invisible summit. This is the mantra spoken by the Buddha of the

Mind. The "spiritual mantra" refers to the heart of the mantra. Recite this section of the Shurangama Mantra one hundred and eight times. **After that, they should secure the boundaries and establish the bodhimanda.** One secures the boundaries to the east as far as they extend, to the west as far as they extend, to the south as far as they extend, and to the north as far as they extend. Once the boundaries are secured, the heavenly demons and adherents of external ways are not permitted to enter the enclosed area. Thus, the bodhimanda and platform will not be plagued by demonic deeds. In this way, the platform, the bodhimanda, is established.

Sutra:

"In the countries within them, they should seek for the unsurpassed Thus Come Ones throughout the ten directions to emit a light of great compassion and anoint the crowns of their heads.

Commentary:

As they recite a hundred and eight times and establish the bodhimanda, **in the countries within them, they should seek for the unsurpassed Thus Come Ones throughout the ten directions,** that is, in the Buddhalands found within the boundaries, **to emit a light of great compassion and anoint the crowns of their heads.** They should beseech all the Buddhas in the lands of the ten directions contained within the boundaries they have secured, to emit a great, compassionate light to moisten and nourish them on the crowns of their heads.

L2   Because of samadhi one opens wisdom.

Sutra:

"Ananda, when any such pure bhikshus, bhikshunis, or white-robed donors in the Dharma-ending Age who can rid their minds of greed and lust hold the Buddha's pure precepts, and in a bodhimanda make the vows of a bodhisattva and can bathe upon entering each time, and day and night for three weeks without sleep continue this practice of the Way, I will appear before these people in a physical form and rub the crowns of their heads to comfort them and enable them to become enlightened."

Commentary:

Ananda, when any such pure bhikshus, bhikshunis, or white-robed donors in the Dharma-ending Age – at that time there may be pure bhikshus or bhikshunis or laypeople. "Donor" is "danapati" in Sanskrit. The Chinese transliteration divides into a word that means "giving" and the word "to transcend." It refers to those people who protect the Triple Jewel. If such people **can rid their minds of greed and lust,** that is, get rid of sexual desire, **hold the Buddha's pure precepts, and in a bodhimanda make the vows of a bodhisattva**:

1. Living beings are boundless; I vow to save them.
2. Afflictions are endless; I vow to cut them off.
3. Dharma-doors are limitless; I vow to study them completely.
4. The Buddha Way is unsurpassed; I vow to accomplish it.

These are the four vast vows of a bodhisattva.

If these people **can bathe upon entering each time, and day and night for three weeks without sleep continue this practice of the Way**. They make the bodhisattva's vows in the bodhimanda, and then they recite the spiritual mantra, the Shurangama Mantra. If they go out, they bathe before they return. Throughout the six periods of the day and night, they practice for three weeks, sitting for three-hour stretches and walking for three-hour stretches. During these twenty-one days and nights, they do not sleep. **I will appear before these people in a physical form and rub the crowns of their heads to comfort them and enable them to become enlightened.** Shakyamuni Buddha says, "I will appear in person before such people and rub the tops of their heads with my hand. I will enable them to obtain the fruition of sagehood."

CHAPTER 2

Establishing the Bodhimanda

G2 At second request he explains in detail.
H1 At second request he describes the bodhimanda.
I1 Ananda asks again.

Sutra:

Ananda said to the Buddha, "World Honored One, enveloped in the Thus Come One's unsurpassed, compassionate instruction, my mind has already become enlightened, and I know how to cultivate and be certified to the path beyond learning. But for those who cultivate in the final age and want to establish a bodhimanda: how do they secure the boundaries in accord with the rules of purity of the Buddha, the World Honored One?"

Commentary:

After Ananda heard what the Buddha had said, he thought to ask about how to secure the boundaries and establish the bodhimanda. **Ananda said to the Buddha, "World Honored One, enveloped in the Thus Come One's unsurpassed, compassionate instruction, my mind has already become enlightened, and I know how to cultivate and be certified to the path beyond learning.** I can accomplish the karma in the path of fourth-stage arhatship and beyond. I am capable of this, **but for those who** cultivate in the final age and want to establish a bodhimanda: how do they secure the boundaries in accord with the rules of purity of the Buddha, the World Honored One? In the future, in the Dharma-ending Age, there will be people who want to set up this kind of bodhimanda. How do they secure the boundaries? How do they accord with your pure rules in doing it, Buddha?"

I2 The World Honored One answers again.
J1 Establishing the bodhimanda.
K1 The platform.

Sutra:

The Buddha said to Ananda, "If there are people in the Dharma-ending Age who wish to establish a bodhimanda, they should first find a powerful white ox in snowy mountains, one which eats the lush and fertile sweet-smelling grasses of the mountain. Since such an ox also drinks only the pure water of the snowy mountains, its excrement will be very fine. They can take that excrement, mix it with chandana, and plaster the ground with it.

Commentary:

Shakyamuni Buddha, having heard Ananda ask about the method for securing the boundaries in accord with the Buddha's rules, **said to Ananda, "If there are people in the Dharma-ending Age who wish to establish a bodhimanda, they should first find a powerful white ox in snowy mountains, one which eats the lush and fertile sweet-smelling grasses of the mountain. Since such an ox also drinks only the pure water of the snowy mountains, its excrement will be very fine. They can take that excrement, mix it with chandana, and plaster the ground with it."** The grasses eaten by the ox are fragrant and so its excrement can be mixed with powdered chandana incense for smearing on the ground.

Sutra:

"If it is not in the snowy mountains, the ox's excrement will stink and cannot be used to smear on the ground. In that case, select a level place, dig down five feet or so, and use that yellow earth.

Commentary:

If it is not in the snowy mountains, the ox's excrement will stink. If the ox does not reside in snowy mountains, it will smell bad and be impure and so its excrement **cannot be used to smear on the ground. In that case, select a level place, dig down five feet or so, and use that yellow earth.** In that case, you should select a flat place, dig down about five feet, and take the yellow earth at that level.

Sutra:

"Mix it with chandana incense, sinking-in-water incense, jasmine incense, continuously permeating incense, burnished gold incense, white paste incense, green wood incense, fragrant mound incense, sweet pine incense, and chicken-tongue incense. Grind these ten ingredients to a fine powder, make a paste, and smear it on the ground of the platform. The area should be sixteen feet wide and octagonal in shape.

Commentary:

Mix it with chandana incense, sinking-in-water incense (*agaru*), **jasmine incense** (*sumana*), **continuously permeating incense, burnished gold incense** (*kunkuma*), **white paste incense, green wood incense, fragrant mound incense** (*kunduruka*), **sweet pine incense, and chicken-tongue incense.** You mix the yellow earth with these ten kinds of incense. **Grind these ten ingredients to a fine powder, make a paste, and smear it on the ground of the platform. The area should be sixteen feet wide and octagonal in shape.**

K2 The adornments.

Sutra:

"In the center of the platform, place a lotus flower made of gold, silver, copper, or wood. In the middle of the flower set a bowl in which dew that has collected in the eighth lunar month has been poured. Let an abundance of flower petals float on the water. Arrange eight circular mirrors in each direction around the flower and the bowl. Outside the mirrors place sixteen lotus flowers and sixteen censers, so that the incense-burners are adorned and arranged between the flowers. Burn only sinking-in-water incense, and do not let the fire be 'seen.'

Commentary:

In the center of the platform, place a lotus flower made of gold, silver, copper, or wood. In the middle of the flower set a bowl in which dew that has collected in the eighth lunar month has been poured. Let an abundance of flower petals float on the water. Arrange eight circular mirrors in each direction around the flower and the bowl. Prepare eight circular mirrors and set them around the bowl of flowers so that they correspond to the eight directions, since it is an octagonal platform. **Outside the mirrors place sixteen lotus flowers and sixteen censers, so that the incense-burners are adorned and arranged between the flowers.** The sixteen flowers and the sixteen censers are placed alternately around the platform. The incense-burners should be adorned so they are pleasing to look at. **Burn only sinking-in-water incense, and do not let the fire be "seen."** In the censers, burn this one kind of incense only. "Do not let the fire be 'seen'" means that the mirror and the flowers should not "see" the fire. In other words, the incense should be lit inside the censer such that the flame is not "visible" in the mirrors or to the flowers.

K3 The offerings.

Sutra:

"Place the milk of a white ox in sixteen vessels, along with cakes made with the milk, rock-candy, oil-cakes, porridge, turushka, honeyed ginger, clarified butter, and filtered honey. These sixteen are set around the outside of the sixteen flowers as an offering to the Buddhas and great bodhisattvas.

Commentary:

Place the milk of a white ox in sixteen vessels, along with cakes made with the milk. Some of the milk is mixed with flour and made into cakes. Also placed in the vessels are **rock-candy, oil-cakes, porridge** – a gruel made with milk and rice – **turushka** incense, **honeyed ginger, clarified butter, and filtered honey. These sixteen are set around the outside of the sixteen flowers.** Place one of the vessels in front of each flower, so that each has one, making sixteen in all. These are **an offering to the Buddhas and great bodhisattvas.**

Sutra:

"At every mealtime and at midnight, prepare a half-pint of honey and three tenths of a pint of clarified butter. Set up a small incense burner in front of the platform. Decoct the fragrant liquid from the turushka incense and use it to cleanse the coals. Light them so that a blaze bursts forth, and toss the clarified butter and honey into the flaming censer. Let it burn until the smoke disappears, and present it to the Buddhas and Bodhisattvas.

Commentary:

At every mealtime and at midnight – it should be done during the day at mealtimes and also at midnight – **prepare a half-pint of honey and three tenths of a pint of clarified butter. Set up a small incense burner in front of the platform.** This is yet another burner, apart from the ones on the platform. It is placed in front of the platform. **Decoct the fragrant liquid from turushka incense and use it to cleanse the coals.** All the charcoal used in the burner should first be washed with the fragrant liquid obtained from turushka, a very fragrant incense. **Light them so that a blaze bursts forth.** Light the burner so that the fire is strong and hot. **Toss the clarified butter and honey into the flaming censer. Let it burn until the smoke disappears, and present it to the Buddhas and Bodhisattvas.** Take the end-product and offer it to the Buddhas and Bodhisattvas.

There are a lot of things like this in the Secret school. They often burn combinations of honey and butter and offer them to the Buddhas. They burn not only that, but anything else of value, such as gold, jewels, and other valuable materials. They first burn them and then offer them to the Buddhas.

Sutra:

"**About the four outside walls one should suspend flags and flowers, and within the room where the platform is located, one should arrange on the four walls images of the Thus Come Ones and bodhisattvas of the ten directions.**

Commentary:

About the four outside walls one should suspend flags and flowers. This refers to the four outer walls of the room in which the platform is located. **And within the room where the platform is located, one should arrange on the four walls images of the Thus Come Ones and bodhisattvas of the ten directions.**

Sutra:

"**In the most prominent place, display images of Vairocana Buddha, Shakyamuni Buddha, Maitreya Bodhisattva, Akshobhya Buddha, Amitabha Buddha, and all the magnificent transformations of Guan Yin Bodhisattva. To the left and right, place the Vajra-Treasury Bodhisattvas. Beside them display the lords Shakra and Brahma, Ucchushma, and the Blue Dirgha, as well as Kundalin and Bhrukuti and all four heavenly kings, with Vinayaka to the left and right of the door.**

Commentary:

In the most prominent place, display images of Vairocana Buddha, Shakyamuni Buddha, Maitreya Bodhisattva, Akshobhya Buddha, Amitabha Buddha, and all the magnificent transformations of Guan Yin Bodhisattva. Vairocana means "pervading all places." Maitreya Bodhisattva is the next Buddha, the Buddha-to-be. He is the plump bodhisattva. Akshobhya Buddha is in the east; he is also known as Medicine Master Buddha. Akshobhya means "unmoving." The east is usually associated with movement, but the Buddha of the east is unmoving. Amitabha means "limitless light" and "limitless life." As to the magnificent transformations of Guan Yin Bodhisattva, we have heard about them already in this sutra, in the passage that said the bodhisattva may have one head, three heads, five heads, seven heads, nine heads, eleven heads, or one hundred and eight heads. It said he may have one hand, three hands, five hands, seven hands, nine hands, as many as one hundred and eight hands, a thousand hands, ten thousand hands, or eighty-four thousand hands. **To the left and right, place the Vajra Treasury Bodhisattvas,** the dharma protectors. They have stern countenances, often terrifying to behold. **Beside them display the lords Shakra and Brahma.** Shakra is the lord of the Heaven of the Thirty-three. He is known as God Almighty, or the Heavenly Lord. Brahma is lord of the Great Brahma Heaven. Also display **Ucchushma and the Blue Dirgha as well as Kundalin and Bhrukuti.** Ucchushma is "Fire-head Vajra." Blue Dirgha has a blue face and is a dharma protector. Kundalin means "releasing the knots of resentment"; it is another name for a vajra spirit. Bhrukuti is also a dharma protector. Display as well images of **all four heavenly kings, with Vinayaka to the left and right of the door.** Vinayaka is another dharma protector who is particularly ugly and frightening. The Chinese description is of two beings, dharma protector Pin Na, who has a human body and a boar's head, and dharma protector Ye Jia who has a human body and an elephant's head and a long trunk. The Indian depictions show Vinayaka, identified with the god Ganesha (*Ganapati*), as one being possessing a human body with an elephant head. Vinayaka also appears as two standing beings with human bodies and elephant heads; the transformation into such bizarre appearances is intentional in order to instill fear in people so they will behave themselves. At the door of the bodhimanda, then, these images are placed on both sides for protection.

K4 The mirrors.

Sutra:

"**Then suspend eight mirrors in the space around the platform so that they are exactly opposite the mirrors on the platform. This will allow the reflections in them to interpenetrate ad infinitum.**

Commentary:

Then suspend eight mirrors in the space around the platform so that they are exactly opposite the mirrors on the platform. "How can they be hung in space?" you wonder. Just as one hangs a lamp from the ceiling. How could one hang them in space alone like the sun? That's not what's meant here. The meaning is to hang them so that they are suspended in the space in the room. The mirrors are placed facing one another. **This will allow the reflections in them to interpenetrate ad infinitum.** That means that the image in one is caught in the other, and within that the image of the interpenetration is shown, and so on, layer within layer in never-ending succession.

J2 Stages of cultivation and accomplishment.
K1 First three weeks: initial accomplishment of samadhi and wisdom.

Sutra:

"**During the first seven days, bow sincerely to the Thus Come Ones of the ten directions, to the great bodhisattvas, and to the names of the arhats. Throughout the six periods of the day and night, continually recite the mantra as you circumambulate the platform. Practice the Way with a sincere mind, reciting the mantra one hundred and eight times at a stretch.**

Commentary:

"**During the first seven days, bow sincerely to the Thus Come Ones of the ten directions, to the great bodhisattvas, and to the names of the arhats. Throughout the six periods of the day and night, continually recite the mantra as you circumambulate the platform.** "The mantra" here is the entire Shurangama

Mantra. **Practice the Way with a sincere mind, reciting the mantra one hundred and eight times at a stretch.** "A sincere mind" means that you don't think of anything else; you single-mindedly hold to the mantra. Each time you recite, go through the mantra one hundred and eight times without stopping.

Sutra:

"During the second week, direct your intent by making the vows of a bodhisattva. The mind should never be cut off from them. In my vinaya, I have already taught about vows.

Commentary:

During the second week of practice, **direct your intent by making the vows of a bodhisattva.** You must be ever more sincere and concentrated. Make the four vast vows of a bodhisattva:

1. Living beings are boundless; I vow to save them.
2. Afflictions are endless; I vow to cut them off.
3. Dharma-doors are limitless; I vow to study them completely.
4. The Buddha Way is unsurpassed; I vow to accomplish it.

The mind should never be cut off from them. This means the mind never stops reciting the Shurangama Mantra, and it never ceases to bring forth the four vast vows. **In my vinaya, I have already taught about vows.** When I spoke the precepts, I taught the practice of making vows.

Sutra:

"During the third week, one holds the Buddha's mantra, Bwo Da La, for twelve hours at a time, with a single intent; and on the seventh day, the Thus Come Ones of the ten directions will appear simultaneously. Their light will be mutually reflected in the mirrors and will illumine the entire place; and they will rub one on the crown of one's head.

Commentary:

During the third week, one holds the Buddha's mantra, Bwo Da La for twelve hours at a time, with a single intent. One holds and recites the mantra "Syi Dan Dwo Bwo Da La," spoken by the Buddha, that is, the Shurangama Mantra. **On the seventh day, the Thus Come Ones of the ten directions will appear simultaneously.** They will suddenly appear in the bodhimanda all at the same time. **Their light will be mutually reflected in the mirrors and will illumine the entire place, and they will rub one on the crown of one's head.** You will have the crown of your head rubbed by the Buddhas of the ten directions, and this act will be reflected within the facing mirrors in a bright image which repeats itself ad infinitum.

Sutra:

"If one cultivates this samadhi in the bodhimanda, then even in the Dharma-ending Age one can study and practice until one's body and mind are as pure and clear as vaidurya.

Commentary:

If one cultivates this samadhi in the bodhimanda with a platform as described above, and if the Thus Come Ones of the ten directions appear simultaneously and aid one by rubbing one on the crown of the head, and if in this way one can practice samadhi, cultivating the return of the hearing to hear the self-nature, **then even in the Dharma-ending Age one can study and practice until one's body and mind are as pure and clear as vaidurya.** One's body and mind will become as transparent as crystal and will shine with light.

K2 After one hundred more days: sudden certification to the sagely fruit.

Sutra:

"Ananda, if any one of the bhikshu's precept transmitting masters or any one of the other bhikshus practicing with him is not pure, the bodhimanda as described will not be successful.

Commentary:

Ananda, if any one of the bhikshu's precept transmitting masters or any one of the other bhikshus practicing with him is not pure, then **the bodhimanda as described will not be successful.** Ananda, you should know that if the bhikshu who is cultivating and upholding this method with the Shurangama Mantra had even one precept-transmitting master who was not pure, or if he is cultivating this practice with another bhikshu who is not pure, then the method will not be successful. It won't work if any one of these people is impure, that is, if they don't hold the precepts purely. Perhaps they hold the precepts and yet violate them. One is not supposed to kill, but they have killed; or one is not supposed to steal, but they have stolen; one is not supposed to commit acts of deviant sexual conduct and they have done so; or one is not supposed to lie, but they have lied. The Buddha taught us not to lie, but they dispense with the "not" and just hold to the "lie." If that is how it is, the bodhimanda will not be successful. All the work of cultivating, all the mantras you held, will still not bring you success. Therefore, if you practice this method and do not get a response from your cultivation, you cannot say, "I cultivated for three weeks, but Shakyamuni Buddha and the Buddhas of the ten directions did not come and rub me on the crown of the head. I didn't even see them. Probably Shakyamuni Buddha was also lying." That is not the case. Perhaps you yourself are not pure, or the teachers from whom you received the precepts were not pure, or any one of the ten people you are practicing this method with may not be pure. If there is even one impure person involved, this state will not be accomplished. This is extremely important.

Sutra:

"After three weeks, one sits upright and still for a hundred days. Those with sharp faculties will not arise from their seats and will become Shrotaapannas. Although their bodies and minds have not attained the ultimate fruition of sagehood, they know for certain, beyond exaggeration, that they will eventually accomplish Buddhahood.

Commentary:

After three weeks, one sits upright and still for a hundred days. One sits in meditation, but not like some people who sit still for two hours and consider it a superb feat. They consider themselves to be outstanding people, but actually, if we compare that to what is described here, it's like a kitten encountering a lion. "Upright" means that one does not lean to the left or right, or lean forward or back, or get up or stretch out one's legs. It's not sitting there and thinking, "Ah my legs really hurt!" Sitting "still" means that nothing troubles one. Sitting for a hundred days means one does not go eat or even get up to relieve oneself. One simply sits for one hundred days. **Those with sharp faculties will not arise from their seats and will become Shrotaapannas.** People who are intelligent and have good roots can then sit for one hundred days and be certified to the first stage of arhatship. But now you can't even sit still for one whole day, and yet there are some who think they have reached the fruition of a sage. That's really ridiculous. You have to be able to sit for a hundred days to accomplish first-stage arhatship. **Although their bodies and minds have not attained the ultimate fruition of sagehood, they know for certain, beyond exaggeration, that they will eventually accomplish Buddhahood.** They still have not attained genuine samadhi power in their cultivation, but they know for a fact that they will certainly become Buddhas. It is definitely not a false notion.

K3 Concludes answer to question.

Sutra:

"You have asked how the bodhimanda is established. This is the way it is done."

Commentary:

This is how you set it up.

CHAPTER 3

The Spiritual Mantra

H2 On second request he speaks the spiritual mantra.
I1 The entire assembly asks again.

Sutra:

Ananda bowed at the Buddha's feet and said, "After I left the home-life, I relied on the Buddha's affectionate regard. Because I sought erudition, I still have not been certified to the unconditioned.

Commentary:

After **Ananda** heard this description by Shakyamuni Buddha, he **bowed at the Buddha's feet and said, "After I left the home-life, I relied on the Buddha's affectionate regard.** I counted on the Buddha's fondness for me, on his special affection. **Because I sought erudition, I still have not been certified to the unconditioned."** He was always concerned about being better than everyone else. "I wanted to surpass others," and so he had the idea, "You can't recite the sutra from memory, but I can. You can't even explain that sutra, and I remember every word of it." He was always competing to be number one. He decided to use erudition to obtain the first position. True enough, Ananda became foremost in learning, but he still did not certify to the unconditioned. He still had not reached to the fruition of sagehood that was unconditioned.

He couldn't obtain the level beyond learning. This was of great harm to him.

Sutra:

"When I encountered that Brahma Heaven mantra, I was captured by the deviant spell; though my mind was aware, I had no power to free myself. I had to rely on Manjushri Bodhisattva to liberate me. Although I was blessed by the Thus Come One's spiritual mantra of the Buddha's summit and imperceptibly received its strength, I still have not heard it myself.

Commentary:

"**When I encountered that Brahma Heaven mantra, I was captured by the deviant spell; though my mind was aware, I had no power to free myself.** I became confused by the deviant spell of the externalist way, by the deviant trick of a demonic devise. I was physically captured by the spell; my body was confused by it, but my mind was still somewhat clear." His mind was not totally alert, but he wasn't totally muddled, either. He was in a daze, as if he were asleep, and yet he was awake. He was as if drunk, but he hadn't taken anything intoxicating. But the effect was much the same as with drink. When you ask a person who has recovered from a drunken binge what he did while under the influence, he will remember some things and forget others. That's the state Ananda was in. Or he was like a person who is about to drift off to sleep; he isn't quite asleep, and yet he has a dream, or what seems to be a dream. He had no power to free himself. It's like encountering a demonic ghost while you are asleep at night, such as a kumbhanda ghost, which uses a demonic spell to paralyze you. When that happens, you may wake up and stare, but you cannot move. You are held by the demonic power of the ghost. That's what Ananda experienced. Although he was conscious, he was not in control of himself. He could not get free. "**I had to rely on Manjushri Bodhisattva to liberate me.** The Buddha commanded Manjushri Bodhisattva to come and save me. I depended on the Buddha to have Manjushri Bodhisattva rescue me. He freed me.

"**Although I was blessed by the Thus Come One's spiritual mantra of the Buddha's summit and imperceptibly received its strength, I still have not heard it myself.** The World Honored One, the Thus Come One, the Buddha, used the spiritual mantra spoken by the transformation Buddha atop the Buddha's summit. And when Manjushri Bodhisattva came to where I was and recited the mantra, I received the benefit invisibly." That means that when Manjushri Bodhisattva got there, he didn't chant the mantra in a loud voice; he merely had to recite it silently to free Ananda. It's all right to recite the mantra loudly when you are before the Buddhas in the temple, but when you are out at other places, you can recite it silently and it is just as effective. If you got out on the streets and start bellowing, "*Na Mwo Sa Dan Two Su Chye Dwo Ye...*" people are going to think you are crazy. You needn't be attached to some particular ritual and thereby cause people to slander the dharma, which is what they would be doing if they said you were crazy. When they commit slander, they commit offenses. You don't want to say, "If he commits offenses, that's his problem. I'll recite even louder and let him slander even more so that he commits even greater offenses, and he will surely fall into the hells." If you have that kind of attitude and intentionally cause people to commit offenses so that they fall into the hells, then you shouldn't even study the Buddhadharma.

People who study the Buddhadharma are sympathetic and compassionate toward others. Their attitude is to do nothing that would cause anyone else to fall into the hells, even to the point that they would rather go to the hells themselves than cause anyone else to go. That's the way you should be. You cannot think, "He slandered me, let him fall into the hells." Or, "If I have a run-in with someone, I will go after them and recite the Shurangama Mantra, and then when they slander me they will fall into the hells." If you have that kind of thought, then you'd better stop reciting the Shurangama Mantra right this minute and leave off your study of the Buddhadharma. That's because people who study the Buddhadharma must not hate people, must not be jealous of people, must not obstruct people, must not be selfish in these ways. One cannot have the attitude, "I'm fine, to heck with you." The Buddhadharma exists for the sake of rescuing all living beings. It is not designed to cause living beings to commit offenses. You must be clear about this point.

Ananda says, "I imperceptibly received its strength, but I still haven't actually heard it. I got the strength from it, but silently and invisibly. So I've never actually heard it. Although I received the benefit of it, I still don't even know how to recite it. I've never even heard it!"

Sutra:

"I only hope that the Greatly Compassionate One will proclaim it again to kindly rescue all the cultivators in this assembly and those of the future who undergo the turning wheel, so that they may become liberated in body and mind by relying on the Buddha's secret sounds."

Commentary:

I only hope that the World Honored One, **the Greatly Compassionate One will proclaim it again.** My one wish is that the Buddha would speak it again so that I can hear it and also **to kindly rescue all the cultivators in this assembly.** Please speak it also to rescue **those of the future who undergo the turning wheel** of the six paths, **so that they may become liberated in body and mind by relying on the Buddha's secret sounds.** Based on the Buddha's secret syllables, they will become free. They will not be upside-down or confused. We recite the Shurangama Mantra every day just to help people stop being upside-down and confused and to help them stay away from doing things which they clearly know are wrong. For instance, one knows that taking opium is wrong – that it wastes time and dissipates one's energy – yet, one still insists on smoking it. Clearly knowing that the use of marijuana is a violation of the law, still one "must" try it out. Well aware that killing is not right, one still takes the lives of living beings. Knowing without a doubt that indulging in sexual misconduct is not right, one conducts oneself in this way nonetheless. Knowing full well that it is wrong to steal, one spends all day and night taking things from other people – if it's not a car, it's a tape-recorder or a radio. A thief knows full well he is breaking the law, and that if he is caught the police will take him to jail, but still he goes and does it. That's "doing things which they clearly know are wrong."

Sutra:

At that moment, everyone in the great assembly bowed as one and stood waiting to hear the Thus Come One's secret divisions and phrases.

Commentary:

At that moment, everyone in the great assembly, the huge multitude of beings in that gathering, **bowed as one and stood waiting to hear the Thus Come One's secret divisions and phrases.** They all bowed together to the Buddha and then stood on tiptoe waiting for the Buddha to speak the secret sections and divisions of the mantra. "Divisions" refers to the five major sections of the mantra. The "phrases" are smaller parts consisting of several lines each, such as *"Na Mwo Sa Dan Two / Su Chye Dwo Ye / E La He Di / San Myau San Pu Two Sye."* But these divisions and phrases are secret, that is, they are not easy for people to understand. They are "secret" in the sense that people do not share a common knowledge about them. When you recite them, you do not know what advantages you obtain. I do not know what advantages I obtain. Although benefit is obtained, there is no mutual awareness of it among those benefited, nor is there a common understanding of the mantra itself.

I2   The Thus Come One answers again.
J1   He speaks the spiritual mantra.
K1   An appearance of light.

Sutra:

At that time, a hundred brilliant rays sprang from the mound of the flesh on the crown of the World Honored One's head. A thousand-petalled precious lotus arose from amidst

those rays. Upon the precious flower sat the Thus Come One's transformation.

Commentary:

At that time, a hundred brilliant rays sprang from the mound of the flesh on the crown of the World Honored One's – Shakyamuni Buddha's – **head. A thousand-petalled precious lotus arose from amidst those rays. Upon the precious flower sat the Thus Come One's transformation.** A transformation body of the Buddha sat upon the thousand-petalled precious lotus in the midst of the hundred rays of light.

Sutra:

From the crown of that Buddha's head, in turn, ten beams of light shone forth, each composed of a hundred rays of precious light. Every one of those glowing rays shone on lands as many as the sands of ten Ganges Rivers, while throughout empty space there were Vajra Secret Traces spirits, each holding aloft a mountain and wielding a pestle.

Commentary:

From the crown of that Buddha's head, in turn, ten beams of light shone forth, each composed of a hundred rays of precious light. "Crown" here refers to the crown of the head of the Thus Come One's transformation. Another ten beams of light issued forth out the top of the head of the transformation-body Buddha. **Every one of those glowing rays shone on lands as many as the sands of ten Ganges Rivers.** These rays of light shone everywhere – on countless countries, **while throughout empty space there were Vajra Secret Traces spirits, each holding aloft a mountain and wielding a pestle.** At the same time that the light shone forth, the Vajra Secret Traces dharma protectors held mountains in their bare hands and brandished pestles, like the one Wei Tuo Bodhisattva wields. They were all over the place, filling up all of empty space.

| K2 | The great assembly respectfully listens. |

Sutra:

The great assembly, gazing upward, felt fearful admiration and sought the Buddha's kind protection. Single-mindedly they listened as the Thus Come One in the light at the invisible appearance on the crown of the Buddha's head proclaimed the spiritual mantra:

Commentary:

The great assembly, gazing upward, felt fearful admiration and sought the Buddha's kind protection. All the great bodhisattvas, great arhats, great bhikshus, and all the others in the great gathering, threw back their heads and looked up toward the transformation-body of the Thus Come One atop the crown of the Buddha's head. Some felt fearful when they saw the transformation Buddha. But at the same time, they admired that Thus Come One. They loved him, but not with the emotional love that exists between men and women. What they felt was true love, free of desire or longing. They had both these feelings at the same time – they were awestruck and yet drawn by love. So they hoped the Buddha would take pity on them and also protect them. **Single-mindedly they listened as the Thus Come One in the light at the invisible appearance on the crown of the Buddha's head proclaimed the spiritual mantra.** They were all of one mind. They all wanted to listen to the Buddha. The mound of flesh on the crown of the Buddha's head is called the "invisible appearance on the crown." It is called the "invisible appearance" because ordinary people cannot see it. Those who saw the hundred rays of light and the transformation Buddha atop the crown of the Buddha's head were sages who had been certified to the fruition. The transformation Buddha that was emitted from the invisible appearance on the crown hovered in space and proclaimed the spiritual mantra.

So, the Shurangama Mantra was not spoken by Shakyamuni Buddha himself in the flesh, but rather it was proclaimed by the transformation-body Buddha he sent out into empty space.

As to the mantra, no one understands it. Nor is it possible to explain it syllable by syllable and line by line. But if you want to understand it, I can try to explain it for you. However, this is not the time for that, because we are in the middle of the explanation of the *Shurangama Sutra*, and the mantra alone couldn't be completely explained in a year, or even in three years, or even ten years. So, at this point it cannot be explained thoroughly. I will simply explain the general meaning of the mantra.

The mantra has five divisions which correspond to the five directions – north, south, east, west, and the middle. The eastern division is the Vajra division, with Akshobhya Buddha as the teaching host. The southern division is the Production-of-Jewels division, with Production-of-Jewels Buddha as the teaching host. The central division is the Buddha division, with Shakyamuni Buddha as the teaching host. The western division is the Lotus division, with Amitabha Buddha as the teaching host. The northern division is the Karma division, with Accomplishment Buddha as the teaching host. There are five divisions because there are five huge demonic armies in this world. There are demons to the east, south, west, north, and in the center. Since there are these five demon armies, not just five demons, the Buddhas also cover the five directions to suppress the demons. If there were no Buddhas, the demons could appear openly in the world.

Within the five divisions of the mantra there are, in general, more than thirty sections, and it has more than a hundred functions that can be discussed in detail. There are five major kinds of functions:

1) The function of bringing accomplishment. This means that with this dharma, you will be successful in what you seek or in what you vow or wish for.

2) The function of increasing benefits. This means that when you recite this mantra, you can increase benefits which you yourself seek and you can also increase benefits for other people.

3) The function of hooking and summoning. This means, literally, to "hook in" and catch and to call with a command all the weird beings, demons, and ghosts. No matter how far away they might be from you, you can bring them in and capture them. For instance, suppose one of them is harming someone, and when they finish they run away. If one knows how to use the function of hooking and summoning, then no matter how far that being may have run, you can arrest him.

4) The function of subduing. Demons also have spiritual penetrations and mantras which they use. When you recite your mantras, they recite their mantras. But if you can use the Shurangama Mantra, you can smash through all their mantras. I've told you before about the section of the mantra which is for smashing the demon kings. It is also effective in destroying their mantras and spells. Although I have taught you this already, it bears repeating here. Those who have not studied this yet can take note of it. Why was it that as soon as the Shurangama Mantra was recited the former Brahma Heaven mantra lost its effectiveness? It was because of the "Five Great Heart Mantras."

> Chr Two Ni
> E Jya La
> Mi Li Ju
> Bwo Li Dan La Ye
> Ning Jye Li

These five lines are called the "Five Great Heart Mantras." It is the fundamental mantra for destroying the mantras and spells of the heavenly demons and adherents of externalist ways. It doesn't matter what kind of mantra they come up with; you can destroy it with this one. Their mantras will lose their effectiveness. This teaching I have just transmitted could sell for several million dollars, but I do not sell it. Seeing that you have a certain amount of sincerity, I transmit it to you absolutely free.

5) The function of dispelling disasters. Whatever calamity is due to occur can be prevented. For instance, suppose a person was

due to fall into the sea and drown, but by reciting the Shurangama Mantra, he avoids the catastrophe. He might fall into the sea, but he doesn't drown. Perhaps you are in a boat that ought to sink, but you recite this mantra and the boat does not go down. Maybe you're in an airplane that is destined to crash, but you recite the Shurangama Mantra and the plane lands without incident. I'll tell you something incredible. I was going from Burma to Thailand, an air route that is particularly dangerous. But during that trip, the plane didn't show the effects of any turbulence. The ride was absolutely smooth. Even the pilot commented, "Why has it been such smooth going on this trip?" He had no idea that during that ride the gods, dragons, and the rest of the eightfold division, as well as Buddhas and Bodhisattvas, were on all sides of the airplane guarding and protecting it.

That's the way the function of dispelling disasters works. When there should clearly be an accident, it can change big disasters to small ones and make small ones never even happen. Usually what happens is there's "alarm but no danger" if you recite the Shurangama Mantra.

In general, the mantra contains functions that bring auspiciousness. This means that when you recite the Shurangama Mantra, everything goes just as you'd like it to. It's really lucky and extremely auspicious.

The advantages of the mantra are so many that one could not even begin to express them in several years time. But at this time, I'll limit my explanation to these few functions and meanings.

K3   The five sections of the spiritual mantra.

Sutra:

I.

na mwo sa dan two
su chye dwo ye
e la he di
san myau san pu two sye
na mwo sa dan two

fwo two jyu jr shai ni shan
na mwo sa pe
bwo two bwo di
sa dwo pi bi
na mwo sa dwo nan
san myau san pu two
jyu jr nan
swo she la pe jya
seng chye nan
na mwo lu ji e lwo han dwo nan
na mwo su lu dwo bwo nwo nan
na mwo swo jye li two chye mi nan
na mwo lu ji san myau chye dwo nan
san myau chye be la
di bwo dwo nwo nan
na mwo ti pe li shai nan
na mwo syi two ye
pi di ye
two la li shai nan
she pwo nu
jya la he
swo he swo la mwo two nan
na mwo ba la he mwo ni
na mwo yin two la ye
na mwo pe chye pe di
lu two la ye
wu bwo be di
swo syi ye ye
na mwo pe chye pe di
nwo la ye

na ye
pan je mwo he san mwo two la
na mwo syi jye li dwo ye
na mwo pe chye pe di
mwo he jya la ye
di li bwo la na
chye la pi two la
bwo na jya la ye
e di mu di
shr mwo she nwo ni
pe syi ni
mwo dan li chye na
na mwo syi jye li dwo ye
na mwo pe chye pe di
dwo two chye dwo jyu la ye
na mwo be tou mwo jyu la ye
na mwo ba she la jyu la ye
na mwo mwo ni jyu la ye
na mwo chye she jyu la ye
na mwo pe chye pe di
di li cha
shu la syi na
bwo la he la na la she ye
dwo two chye dwo ye
na mwo pe chye pe di
na mwo e mi dwo pe ye
dwo two chye dwo ye
e la he di
san myau san pu two ye
na mwo pe chye pe di

e chu pi ye
dwo two chye dwo ye
e la he di
san myau san pu two ye
na mwo pe chye pe di
bi sha she ye
jyu lu fei ju li ye
bwo la pe la she ye
dwo two chye dwo ye
na mwo pe chye pe di
san bu shr bi dwo
sa lyan nai la la she ye
dwo two chye dwo ye
e la he di
san myau san pu two ye
na mwo pe chye pe di
she ji ye mu nwo ye
dwo two chye dwo ye
e la he di
san myau san pu two ye
na mwo pe chye pe di
la dan na ji du la she ye
dwo two chye dwo ye
e la he di
san myau san pu two ye
di pyau
na mwo sa jye li dwo
yi tan pe chye pe dwo
sa dan two chye du shai ni shan
sa dan dwo bwo da lan

na mwo e pe la shr dan
bwo la di
yang chi la
sa la pe
bwo dwo jye la he
ni jye la he
jye jya la he ni
ba la bi di ye
chr two ni
e jya la
mi li ju
bwo li dan la ye
ning jye li
sa la pe
pan two nwo
mu cha ni
sa la pe
tu shai jya
tu syi fa
bwo na ni
fa la ni
je du la
shr di nan
jye la he
swo he sa la rau she
pi dwo beng swo na jye li
e shai ja bing she di nan
na cha cha dan la rau she
bwo la sa two na jye li
e shai ja nan

mwo he jye la he rau she
pi dwo beng sa na jye li
sa pe she du lu
ni pe la rau she
hu lan tu syi fa
nan je na she ni
pi sha she
syi dan la
e ji ni
wu two jya la rau she
e bwo la shr dwo jyu la
mwo he bwo la jan chr
mwo he dye dwo
mwo he di she
mwo he shwei dwo she pe la
mwo he ba la pan two la
pe syi ni
e li ye dwo la
pi li jyu jr
shr pe pi she ye
ba she la mwo li di
pi she lu dwo
bwo teng wang jya
ba she la jr he nwo e je
mwo la jr pe
bwo la jr dwo
ba she la shan chr
pi she la je
shan dwo she
pi ti pe

bu shr dwo
su mwo lu bwo
mwo he shwei dwo
e li ye dwo la
mwo he pe la e bwo la
ba she la shang jye la jr pe
ba she la jyu mwo li
jyu lan two li
ba she la he sa dwo je
pi di ye
chyan je nwo
mwo li jya
ku su mu
pe jye la dwo nwo
pi lu je na
jyu li ye
ye la tu
shai ni shan
pi je lan pe mwo ni je
ba she la jya na jya bwo la pe
lu she na
ba she la dwun jr je
shwei dwo je
jya mwo la
cha che shr
bwo la pe
yi di yi di
mu two la
jye na
swo pi la chan

jywe fan du
yin tu na mwo mwo sye

II.
wu syin
li shai jye na
bwo la she syi dwo
sa dan two
chye du shai ni shan
hu syin du lu yung
jan pe na
hu syin du lu yung
syi dan pe na
hu syin du lu yung
bwo la shai di ye
san bwo cha
na jye la
hu syin du lu yung
sa pe yau cha
he la cha swo
jye la he rau she
pi teng beng sa na jye la
hu syin du lu yung
je du la
shr di nan
jye la he
swo he sa la nan
pi teng beng sa na la
hu syin du lu yung
la cha

pe chye fan
sa dan two
chye du shai ni shan
bwo la dyan
she ji li
mwo he swo he sa la
bwo shu swo he sa la
shr li sha
jyu jr swo he sa ni
di li e bi ti shr pe li dwo
ja ja ying jya
mwo he ba she lu two la
di li pu pe na
man cha la
wu syin
swo syi di
bwo pe du
mwo mwo
yin tu na mwo mwo sye

III.
la she pe ye
ju la be ye
e chi ni pe ye
wu two jya pe ye
pi sha pe ye
she sa dwo la pe ye
pe la jau jye la pe ye
tu shai cha pe ye
e she ni pe ye

e jya la
mi li ju pe ye
two la ni bu mi jyan
bwo chye bwo two pe ye
wu la jya pe dwo pe ye
la she tan cha pe ye
nwo chye pe ye
pi tyau dan pe ye
su bwo la na pe ye
yau cha jye la he
la cha sz jye la he
bi li dwo jye la he
pi she je jye la he
bu dwo jye la he
jyou pan cha jye la he
bu dan na jye la he
jya ja bu dan na jye la he
syi chyan du jye la he
e bwo syi mwo la jye la he
wu tan mwo two jye la he
che ye jye la he
syi li pe di jye la he
she dwo he li nan
jye pe he li nan
lu di la he li nan
mang swo he li nan
mi two he li nan
mwo she he li nan
she dwo he li nyu
shr bi dwo he li nan

pi dwo he li nan
pe dwo he li nan
e shu je he li nyu
jr dwo he li nyu
di shan sa pi shan
sa pe jye la he nan
pi two ye she
chen two ye mi
ji la ye mi
bwo li ba la je jya
chi li dan
pi two ye she
chen two ye mi
ji la ye mi
cha yan ni
chi li dan
pi two ye she
chen two ye mi
ji la ye mi
mwo he bwo su bwo dan ye
lu two la
chi li dan
pi two ye she
chen two ye mi
ji la ye mi
nwo la ye na
chi li dan
pi two ye she
chen two ye mi
ji la ye mi

dan two chye lu cha syi
chi li dan
pi two ye she
chen two ye mi
ji la ye mi
mwo he jya la
mwo dan li chye na
chi li dan
pi two ye she
chen two ye mi
ji la ye mi
jya bwo li jya
chi li dan
pi two ye she
chen two ye mi
ji la ye mi
she ye jye la
mwo du jye la
sa pe la two swo da na
chi li dan
pi two ye she
chen two ye mi
ji la ye mi
je du la
pe chi ni
chi li dan
pi two ye she
chen two ye mi
ji la ye mi
pi li yang chi li jr

nan two ji sha la
chye na bwo di
swo syi ye
chi li dan
pi two ye she
chen two ye mi
ji la ye mi
na jye na she la pe na
chi li dan
pi two ye she
chen two ye mi
ji la ye mi
e lwo han
chi li dan
pi two ye she
chen two ye mi
ji la ye mi
pi dwo la chye
chi li dan
pi two ye she
chen two ye mi
ji la ye mi
ba she la bwo ni
jyu syi ye jyu syi ye
jya di bwo di
chi li dan
pi two ye she
chen two ye mi
ji la ye mi
la cha wang

pe chye fan
yin tu na mwo mwo sye

IV.
pe chye fan
sa dan dwo bwo da la
na mwo tswei du di
e syi dwo na la la jya
bwo la pe
syi pu ja
pi jya sa dan dwo be di li
shr fwo la shr fwo la
two la two la
pin two la pin two la
chen two chen two
hu syin hu syin
pan ja pan ja pan ja pan ja pan ja
swo he
syi syi pan
e mu jye ye pan
e bwo la ti he dwo pan
pe la bwo la two pan
e su la
pi two la
bwo jya pan
sa pe ti pi bi pan
sa pe na chye bi pan
sa pe yau cha bi pan
sa pe chyan ta pe bi pan
sa pe bu dan na bi pan

jya ja bu dan na bi pan
sa pe tu lang jr di bi pan
sa pe tu sz bi li
chi shai di bi pan
sa pe shr pe li bi pan
sa pe e bwo syi mwo li bi pan
sa pe che la pe na bi pan
sa pe di di ji bi pan
sa pe dan mwo two ji bi pan
sa pe pi two ye
la shr je li bi pan
she ye jye la
mwo du jye la
sa pe la two swo two ji bi pan
pi di ye
je li bi pan
je du la
fu chi ni bi pan
ba she la
jyu mwo li
pi two ye
la shr bi pan
mwo he bwo la ding yang
yi chi li bi pan
ba she la shang jye la ye
bwo la jang chi la she ye pan
mwo he jya la ye
mwo he mwo dan li jya na
na mwo swo jye li dwo ye pan
bi shai na bei ye pan

bwo la he mwo ni ye pan
e chi ni ye pan
mwo he jye li ye pan
jye la tan chr ye pan
mye dan li ye pan
lau dan li ye pan
je wen cha ye pan
jye lwo la dan li ye pan
jya bwo li ye pan
e di mu jr dwo
jya shr mwo she nwo
pe sz ni ye pan
yan ji jr
sa two pe sye
mwo mwo yin tu na mwo mwo sye

V.
tu shai ja jr dwo
e mwo dan li jr dwo
wu she he la
chye pe he la
lu di la he la
pe swo he la
mwo she he la
she dwo he la
shr bi dwo he la
ba lyau ye he la
chyan two he la
bu shr bwo he la
pwo la he la

pe sye he la
be bwo jr dwo
tu shai ja jr dwo
lau two la jr dwo
yau cha jye la he
la cha swo jye la he
bi li dwo jye la he
pi she je jye la he
bu dwo jye la he
jyou pan cha jye la he
syi chyan two jye la he
wu dan mwo two jye la he
che ye jye la he
e bwo sa mwo la jye la he
jai chywe ge
cha chi ni jye la he
li fwo di jye la he
she mi jya jye la he
she jyu ni jye la he
mu two la
na di jya jye la he
e lan pe jye la he
chyan du bwo ni jye la he
shr fwo la
yin jya syi jya
jywe di yau jya
dan li di yau jya
je tu two jya
ni ti shr fa la
bi shan mwo shr fa la

bwo di jya
bi di jya
shr li shai mi jya
swo ni bwo di jya
sa pe shr fa la
shr lu ji di
mwo two pi da lu jr jyan
e chi lu chyan
mu chywe lu chyan
jye li tu lu chyan
jya la he
jye lan jye na shu lan
dan dwo shu lan
chi li ye shu lan
mwo mwo shu lan
ba li shr pe shu lan
bi li shai ja shu lan
wu two la shu lan
jye jr shu lan
ba syi di shu lan
wu lu shu lan
chang chye shu lan
he syi dwo shu lan
ba two shu lan
swo fan ang chye
bwo la jang chye shu lan
bu dwo bi dwo cha
cha chi ni
shr pe la
two tu lu jya

jyan du lu ji jr
pe lu dwo pi
sa bwo lu
he ling chye
shu sha dan la
swo na jye la
pi sha yu jya
e chi ni
wu two jya
mwo la pi la
jyan dwo la
e jya la
mi li du
da lyan bu jya
di li la ja
bi li shai jr jya
sa pe na jyu la
sz yin chye bi
jye la li yau cha
dan la chu
mwo la shr
fei di shan
swo pi shan
syi dan dwo bwo da la
mwo he ba she lu
shai ni shan
mwo he bwo lai jang chi lan
ye bwo tu two
she yu she nwo
byan da li na

pi two ye
pan tan jya lu mi
di shu
pan tan jya lu mi
bwo la pi two
pan tan jya lu mi
dwo jr two
nan
e na li
pi she ti
pi la
ba she la
two li
pan two pan two ni
ba she la bang ni pan
hu syin du lu yung pan
swo pe he.

J2 He speaks of the benefits of the mantra.
K1 The important tool of all Buddhas.
L1 He explains the entire name.

Sutra:

"Ananda, this cluster of light atop the crown of the Buddha's head, the secret gatha, Syi Dan Dwo Bwo Da La, with its subtle, wonderful divisions and phrases, gives birth to all the Buddhas of the ten directions. Because the Thus Come Ones of the ten directions use this mantra-heart, they realize unsurpassed, proper, and all-pervading knowledge and enlightenment.

Commentary:

Ananda, this cluster of light atop the crown of the Buddha's head, the secret gatha, Syi Dan Dwo Bwo Da La, is again, the great white canopy, which can cover over the entire system of three thousand great thousand worlds to protect all the living beings in it. "Gatha" is a Sanskrit term which means "repetitive verses." The mantra is secret, and since some of its lines are repeated, it is referred to as the "secret gatha." These "divisions and phrases" which comprise the mantra are extremely rare and miraculous.

This mantra, **with its subtle, wonderful divisions and phrases, gives birth to all the Buddhas of the ten directions.** Therefore, the Shurangama Mantra can be called the "Mother of Buddhas."

Because the Thus Come Ones of the ten directions use this mantra-heart, they realize unsurpassed proper and all-pervading knowledge and enlightenment. It is by means of the Shurangama Mantra that the Buddhas realize proper and all-pervading awareness. "Proper knowledge" means they know that the mind gives rise to the myriad phenomena; "all-pervading knowledge" means that they know that the myriad phenomena comes only from the mind.

L2　He states its functions.

Sutra:

"**Because the Thus Come Ones of the ten directions take up this mantra-heart, they subdue all demons and control all adherents of outside ways.**

Commentary:

The "mantra-heart" – the Shurangama Mantra – was spoken by a transformation body Buddha seated upon a jeweled lotus amidst a thousand rays of light at the crown of the Buddha Shakyamuni's head. **Because the Thus Come Ones of the ten directions take up this mantra-heart, they subdue all demons and control all adherents of outside ways.** It is the heart of mantras, and it is a mantra-heart of the Buddhas. Therefore, what the heavenly demons and adherents of outside ways fear most is the Shurangama Mantra.

Sutra:

"Because the Thus Come Ones of the ten directions avail themselves of this mantra-heart, they sit upon jeweled lotus-flowers and respond throughout countries as numerous as motes of dust.

Commentary:

Because the Thus Come Ones of the ten directions avail themselves of this mantra-heart. They borrow the mantra; as it were, they ascend the mantra-heart, and **they sit upon jeweled lotus-flowers** – huge blossoms – **and respond throughout countries as numerous as motes of dust.** Their response-bodies are able to go throughout lands as numerous as fine motes of dust, due to the power of the Shurangama Mantra-heart.

Sutra:

"Because the Thus Come Ones of the ten directions embody this mantra-heart, they turn the great dharma wheel in lands as numerous as fine motes of dust.

Commentary:

When **the Thus Come Ones of the ten directions turn the great dharma wheel in lands as numerous as fine motes of dust,** they also base themselves on this mantra. **They embody this mantra-heart.**

Sutra:

"Because the Thus Come Ones of the ten directions hold this mantra-heart, they are able to go throughout the ten directions to rub beings on the crowns of their heads and bestow predictions upon them. Also, anyone in the ten directions who has not yet realized the fruition, can receive a Buddha's prediction.

Commentary:

Because the Thus Come Ones of the ten directions hold this mantra-heart – they receive and uphold this mantra-heart, and so **they are able to go throughout the ten directions to rub beings**

on the crowns of their heads and bestow predictions upon them. They bestow predictions of Buddhahood on other living beings. Also, anyone in the ten directions who has not yet realized the fruition, can receive a Buddha's prediction. If you have not realized the fruition, the Buddhas may still rub the crown of your head and bestow a prediction on you.

Sutra:

"Because the Thus Come Ones of the ten directions are based in this mantra-heart, they can go throughout the ten directions to rescue beings from such sufferings as being in the hells, being hungry ghosts, being animals, or being blind, deaf, or mute, as well as from the suffering of being together with those one hates, from the suffering of being apart from those one loves, from the suffering of not obtaining what one seeks, and from the raging blaze of the five skandhas. They liberate beings from both large and small accidents. In response to their recitation, difficulty with thieves, difficulty with armies, difficulty with the law, difficulty with imprisonment, difficulty with wind, fire, and water, and difficulty with hunger, thirst, and impoverishment are all eradicated.

Commentary:

Because the Thus Come Ones of the ten directions are based in this mantra-heart, they can go throughout the ten directions to rescue beings from such sufferings as the eight sufferings:
1. birth,
2. old age,
3. sickness,
4. death,
5. being apart from those one loves,
6. being together with those one hates,
7. being unable to obtain what one seeks,
8. the raging blaze of the five skandhas.

There are also eight difficulties:
1. the difficulty of the hells,
2. the difficulty of hungry ghosts,
3. the difficulty of animals,
4. the difficulty of being blind, deaf, or mute,
5. the difficulty of being in Uttarakuru,
6. the difficulty of being born at a time when there is no Buddha in the world,
7. the difficulty of having worldly intelligence and powers in debate,
8. the difficulty of being reborn in the long-life heavens.

The beings in the northern continent, Uttarakuru, have a very long lifespan. They live an average of a thousand years. Life on that continent is extremely blissful; the difficulty is that the beings there have no opportunity to see the Buddha, hear the Dharma, or meet the Sangha. Therefore, living there is included among the eight difficulties. The same is true for beings in the heavens; although the lifespan is long, they have no chance to encounter the Triple Jewel. So that, too, is a difficulty.

"Having worldly intelligence and powers in debate" refers to different branches of mundane knowledge, such as the fields of science. They try to express principles where there are no principles and to give reasons when there aren't any.

Being in the hells, being hungry ghosts, being animals, or being blind, deaf, or mute, are among the eight difficulties.

Then there is **the suffering of being together with those one hates.** This is when you move to get away from someone you can't stand, only to find that when you get to the new place, there's a person just like him there! There is also **the suffering of being apart from those one loves.** You love someone especially, but circumstances force you to be apart. Again, there is **the suffering of not obtaining what one seeks.** When you don't have something that you want, you seek for it. But if you encounter this suffering, you fail to get what you seek. **The raging blaze of the five skandhas** – form, feeling, thought, activity, and consciousness, the five skandhas, burn like fire.

They liberate beings from both large and small accidents. This can refer to untimely deaths, such as being killed in an automobile accident, being crushed by a falling building, or any other fatal accident. They can also liberate beings from **difficulty with thieves, difficulty with armies, difficulty with the law, difficulty with imprisonment, difficulty with wind, fire, and water, and difficulty with hunger, thirst, and impoverishment. In response to their recitation, all** these difficulties **are eradicated.**

Sutra:

"Because the Thus Come Ones of the ten directions are in accord with this mantra-heart, they can serve good and wise advisors throughout the ten directions. In the four aspects of awesome deportment, they make wish-fulfilling offerings. In the assemblies of as many Thus Come Ones as there are sands in the Ganges, they are considered to be great dharma princes.

Commentary:

Because the Thus Come Ones of the ten directions are in accord with this mantra-heart, they can serve good and wise advisors throughout the ten directions. They respectfully offer up their services to good and wise advisors. **In the four aspects of awesome deportment, they make wish-fulfilling offerings.** In the ceremony of offering to the Triple Jewel, their conduct is perfectly appropriate. **In the assemblies of as many Thus Come Ones as there are sands in the Ganges, they are considered to be great dharma princes.** They are the foremost disciples of the Buddha.

Sutra:

"Because the Thus Come Ones of the ten directions practice this mantra-heart, they can gather in and teach their relatives in the ten directions. Causing those of the small vehicle not to be frightened when they hear the secret treasury.

Commentary:

Because the Thus Come Ones of the ten directions practice this mantra-heart, they can gather in and teach their relatives in the ten directions. Buddhas have the six kinds of close relatives, too, and they first gather in and teach those of their relatives who draw near to them. Why was it that when Shakyamuni Buddha became a Buddha he went first to the Deer Wilds Park to take across the five bhikshus? It is because those five bhikshus were his relatives in that present life and had been his relatives in lives past. They can teach them, **causing those of the small vehicle,** that is, their relatives who have fallen into studying the small vehicle teachings, **not to be frightened when they hear the secret treasury.** When they hear the treasury of secrets told by the Buddha, they are not afraid of the great vehicle teachings.

Sutra:

"Because the Thus Come Ones of the ten directions recite this mantra-heart, they realize unsurpassed enlightenment while sitting beneath the bodhi tree, and they enter parinirvana.

Commentary:

Because the Thus Come Ones of the ten directions recite this mantra-heart. How do the Thus Come Ones in the ten directions become Buddhas? It is also because they recite this mantra-heart. "Recite" means to repeat from memory without looking at the book. **They realize unsurpassed enlightenment while sitting beneath the bodhi tree,** and become Buddhas because they recite this mantra. **And they enter parinirvana.**

Sutra:

"Because the Thus Come Ones of the ten directions transmit this mantra-heart, those to whom they have bequeathed the Buddhadharma can, after their nirvana, dwell in it completely and uphold it. Being strict and pure about the precepts and rules, they can all obtain purity.

Commentary:

Because the Thus Come Ones of the ten directions, transmit this mantra-heart, those to whom they have bequeathed the Buddhadharma can, after their nirvana, dwell in it completely and uphold it. After the Buddhas go to nirvana, people who inherit the dharma from them know how to cultivate and to receive and uphold the Buddhadharma. **Being strict and pure about the precepts and rules, they can all obtain purity.** It is because of the power of the mantra that they obtain purity and perfection.

L3　Further explanations are endless.

Sutra:

"If I were to explain this mantra, Bwo Da La, of the cluster of light atop the crown of the Buddha's head from morning till night in an unceasing sound, without ever repeating any syllable or phrase, I could go on for as many kalpas as there are sands in the Ganges and still never finish.

Commentary:

If I were to explain this mantra, Bwo Da La, of the cluster of light atop the crown of the Buddha's head from morning till night in an unceasing sound, without ever repeating any syllable or phrase. The "mantra Bwo Da La" refers to the Shurangama Mantra, the "durable mantra," the mantra of the great white canopy. **I could go on for as many kalpas as there are sands in the Ganges and still never finish.** I would never come to the end of my explanation of the Shurangama Mantra-heart's merits and virtues and wonderful functions.

K2　A beneficial reliance for living beings.
L1　Specific explanation of the supreme name.

Sutra:

"I also will tell you that this mantra is called 'The Crown of the Thus Come One.'

Commentary:

I also will tell you that this mantra is called "The Crown of the Thus Come One." That's another name for it.

L2 A thorough discussion of its awesome power.
M1 He first explains that by diligently holding it, cultivators can rely on it.
N1 He explains that recitation of it will keep demons away.

Sutra:

"All of you with something left to study who have not yet put an end to the cycle of rebirth and yet have brought forth sincere resolve to become arhats, will find it impossible to sit in a bodhimanda and be far removed in body and mind from all demonic deeds if you do not hold this mantra.

Commentary:

All of you with something left to study who have not yet put an end to the cycle of rebirth are still caught in the turning wheel of the six paths. **And yet you have brought forth sincere resolve to become arhats.** You would like to attain the fruition of arhatship. But you **will find it impossible to sit in a bodhimanda and be far removed in body and mind from all demonic deeds if you do not hold this mantra.** If you want to become an arhat and yet do not hold this mantra, or if you want to sit in a bodhimanda and become a Buddha, and yet have part in demonic activities, either physically or mentally, you are attempting the impossible. In other words, you must recite this mantra to be free of demonic doings. If you don't hold this mantra, you cannot sit in the bodhimanda, nor can you stay away from the deeds of demons.

N2 Writing it out and carrying it is of benefit.

Sutra:

"Ananda, let any living being of any country in any world copy out this mantra in writing on materials native to his region, such as birch bark, pattra, plain paper, or white cotton cloth, and store it in a pouch containing incense. If that person wears the pouch on his body, or if he keeps a copy in his home,

then you should know that even if he understands so little that he cannot recite it from memory, he will not be harmed by any poison during his entire life.

Commentary:

The functions of the mantra are discussed here. **Ananda, let any living being of any country in any world** – this means that in this world or another world or in any one of limitless worlds, a person may **copy out this mantra in writing on materials native to his region.** The person could be American, English, French, German, Japanese, Chinese, Indian, Thai, Burmese, Ceylonese, or a citizen of any other country. Perhaps he writes on **birch bark** or on **pattra**, which are palm leaves, on **plain paper, or white cotton cloth.** Whether he writes it out on paper or cloth or some other material that can be written on doesn't matter. And he can copy it carefully and respectfully, or write it out casually in long-hand. Let him **store it in a pouch containing incense. If that person wears the pouch on his body, or if he keeps a copy in his home, then you should know that even if he understands so little that he cannot recite it from memory, he will not be harmed by any poison during his entire life.** If the person doesn't have a good memory or if he is muddle-headed and can't recite the mantra well, he can write the mantra out and wear it in a little bag, or he can write it out and hang it on the wall of his house. If someone does that, he will go through his entire life without being poisoned. There are strong and weak poisons, but no matter what kind it is, it cannot harm him.

M2 A detailed account of the ways in which it protects life and aids people on the path.
N1 General mention of these two aspects.

Sutra:

"Ananda, I will now tell you more about how this mantra can rescue and protect the world, help people obtain great fearlessness, and bring to accomplishment living beings' transcendental wisdom.

Commentary:

Ananda, I will now tell you more about how this mantra, the Shurangama Mantra, **can rescue and protect the world, help people obtain great fearlessness, and bring to accomplishment living beings' transcendental wisdom.** It can fulfill any wishes living beings might have, but most importantly, it can reveal their transcendental wisdom.

N2 Detailed listing of its many merits.
O1 Apparent benefit to each living being.
P1 Rescues from calamities.
Q1 Evil situations cannot bring harm.

Sutra:

"You should know that, after my extinction, if there are beings in the Dharma-ending Age who can recite the mantra themselves or teach others to recite it, such people who recite and uphold it cannot be burned by fire, cannot be drowned by water, and cannot be harmed by mild or potent poisons.

Commentary:

You should know that, after my extinction, if there are beings in the Dharma-ending Age – this includes you and me – **who can recite the mantra themselves or teach others to recite it, such people who recite and uphold it cannot be burned by fire.** Perhaps one can recite the mantra from memory or teach others to recite it from memory. People who can recite the mantra from memory or can read it will not be burned by fire, and they **cannot be drowned by water,** nor can they **be harmed by mild or potent poisons.**

Q2 Evil beings cannot break through its added protection to cause harm.

Sutra:

"And so it is in every other case, such that they cannot be possessed by any evil mantra or any heavenly dragon, ghost, or spirit, or by any essence, weird creature, or demonic ghost. These people's minds will attain proper reception, so that any

spell, any paralyzing sorcery, any poison or poisoning gold, any poisoning silver, any plant, tree, insect, or snake, and any of a myriad kinds of poisonous vapors will turn into sweet dew when it enters their mouths.

Commentary:

And so it is in every other case, such that they cannot be possessed by any evil mantra or any heavenly dragon, ghost, or spirit, or by any essence, weird creature, or demonic ghost. All these kinds of ghosts and demons use evil spells. The five phrases of the mantra I told you about recently,

> Chr Two Ni
> E Jya La
> Mi Li Ju
> Bwo Li Dan La Ye
> Ning Jye Li

represent the five directions, the five divisions, and the five Buddhas. They are known as the "Five Great Heart Mantras." You should not regard them as ordinary. Together they comprise the heart-mantra of the Buddhas of the five directions. The function of this heart-mantra is to destroy the mantras and spells of demons. It doesn't matter what kind of evil spell they are weaving; you can smash through it with this mantra. Their mantras lose all their effectiveness. They are rendered useless. These evil mantras cannot possess you, because the Five Great Heart Mantras destroys them.

These people's minds will attain proper reception. If you recite the Shurangama Mantra, you can obtain proper concentration, **so that any spell** – any devious mantra of the heavenly demons or of adherents of externalist ways – cannot harm you. **Any paralyzing sorcery.** There is a lot of sorcery in southern China, also in Southeast Asia, such as Burma, Korea, Thailand, Singapore, Malaysia, and such places. The kind of sorcery they use, called *ku* is also based on mantras and spells. If you eat something poisoned by them, you are forever under their spell; you must do as they command. If you don't, you die.

In Australia, in the mountain regions, there is a religious sect that uses mantras to shrink people's heads to the size of chicken eggs. And then they put them on display as sorcerer's charms. In a world as large as this, there are every kind of weird thing unimaginable. You shouldn't have the attitude that if you haven't seen it, you don't believe it exists. If you don't believe it, you're just plain stupid. Why do I say that? There are lots of things you've never seen, and if you go on with the idea that you must see them before you believe them, you'll never finish in your entire life. Before America was discovered, before anyone knew it existed, if you had approached someone and tried to convince him that there was, in fact, another continent with mountains and all the rest, he very likely would not have believed you. But, though he may have denied the existence of America, would that have meant that America did not, in fact, exist? Was it there before it was discovered? Whether or not he admitted its existence, it still existed. By the same token, whether or not you believe that the strange things being discussed here exist, they exist nonetheless. So if you deny the existence of a thing just because you haven't seen it yourself, you basically don't have a grasp of the way the world really is.

If someone sinks some *ku* in you, if they apply their sorcery to you, you are forever their slave. If you oppose them, you die. In addition to *ku* poison, if **any poison or poisoning gold, any poisoning silver, any plant, tree, insect, or snake, or any of a myriad kinds of poisonous vapors enter the mouth** of people who recite the Shurangama Mantra, **it will turn into sweet dew.**

"Suppose I test this," you suggest. "Suppose I experiment." You still haven't perfected your recitation of the Shurangama Mantra. When you've got it down to the point that it's efficacious and magical, then you can experiment. Before you reach that stage, don't play around with it.

Sutra:

"No evil stars, and no ghost or spirit that harbors malice in its heart and that poisons people can work its evil on these people. Vinayaka as well as all the evil ghost kings and their retinues will be led by deep kindness to always guard and protect them.

Commentary:

The previous section of text said that any kind of poisonous thing that enters the mouth of a person who recites and upholds the Shurangama Mantra will turn into sweet dew. These things are basically poisonous, but their composition changes. And the change comes about because one recites and upholds the Shurangama Mantra. **No evil star** refers to evil constellations and such things as *Tai Sui* and the White-tiger Star, which is terrible. And there is the star *Sang Men*, which is extremely inauspicious and can kill people. But none of these kinds of stars can harm one, nor can any **ghost or spirit that harbors malice in its heart and poisons people.** Some people say they don't believe in ghosts or spirits. They have never seen a ghost, and so they don't believe there are any. If they saw one, they'd have no way not to believe in it, even if they didn't want to. "Malice" is also a kind of poison, like arsenic. That drug is fatal if more than a little is taken. But someone with even that much poison in his heart still cannot harm a person who recites and upholds the Shurangama Mantra. He cannot **work his evil on these people.** Rather, the poison in their own hearts is transformed.

Vinayaka was mentioned in the description of setting up the bodhimanda. He is a protector with the various transformations which often show a boar or an elephant head with a trunk on a human body. In general he is extremely ugly. He **as well as the evil ghost kings and their retinues will be led by deep kindness to always guard and protect them.** Having been influenced by the profound compassion of the Buddha in the past, these ghost kings and dharma protectors have resolved to always guard and protect those who recite and uphold the Shurangama Mantra. The advantages of reciting the Shurangama Mantra are truly inconceivable.

P2 Aids in accomplishing way karma.
Q1 The value of its recitation.

Sutra:

"Ananda, you should know that eighty-four thousand nayutas of Ganges' sands of kotis of Vajra Treasury-King Bodhisattvas and their descendants, each with vajra multitudes as retinue, are ever in attendance, day and night, upon this mantra.

Commentary:

"Nayuta" is one of the fourteen large numbers in Sanskrit. Some say it represents one trillion; others say ten trillion. In general, it's a big number. "Ganges' sands of kotis" is said to be equivalent to a trillion. Not only are the Vajra Treasury-King Bodhisattvas in attendance on the mantra, those of their lineage are also present. And each member of the entire lineage is accompanied by a retinue of vajra beings. Day and night, they are always present wherever the Shurangama Mantra is being upheld.

These bodhisattvas are the ones praised in the section above:

>Namo Buddhas of the ten directions,
>Namo Dharma of the ten directions,
>Namo Sangha of the ten directions,
>Namo Shakyamuni Buddha,
>Namo Foremost Shurangama atop the Buddha's summit,
>Namo *Guan Shi Yin* Bodhisattva,
>Namo Vajra Treasury Bodhisattvas.

The eighty-four thousand are referred to in the last line. But actually, it's not only the Vajra Treasury Bodhisattvas who are so numerous. The retinues of all bodhisattvas are that numerous.

Sutra:

"If living beings whose minds are scattered and who have no samadhi remember and recite the mantra, the Vajra Kings will always surround them. Therefore, good men, that is even more

true for those who are decisively resolved upon bodhi. All the Vajra Treasury-King Bodhisattvas will regard them attentively and secretly hasten the opening of their spiritual consciousness.

Commentary:

If living beings whose minds are scattered – their thoughts go every which way and are not the least bit concentrated. They also have **no samadhi** power, but they **remember and recite the mantra**. They remember the Shurangama Mantra spoken by the Buddha. **The Vajra Kings,** the bodhisattvas, **will always surround them,** that is, those with scattered minds, if they uphold the Shurangama Mantra. **Therefore, good men, that is even more true for those who are decisively resolved upon bodhi.** You people who have firmly brought forth the bodhi mind will also be protected by these **Vajra Treasury-King Bodhisattvas,** who **will regard** you **attentively and secretly hasten the opening of** your **spiritual consciousness.** With close regard for you, they will help you in hidden ways. What will they do? They will help you increase your wisdom – your spiritual consciousness. Little by little they will help those who have scattered minds to become concentrated. Gradually they will obtain samadhi power. Invisibly they will help those who hold the mantra to open their wisdom and become single-minded.

Sutra:

"When that response occurs, those people will be able to remember the events of as many kalpas as there are grains of sand in eighty-four thousand Ganges Rivers, knowing them all beyond any doubt.

Commentary:

When the Vajra Treasury-King Bodhisattvas invisibly open their spiritual awareness – **when that response occurs, those people will be able to remember the events of as many kalpas as there are grains of sand in eighty-four thousand Ganges Rivers, knowing them all beyond any doubt.** They know very clearly about everything that took place throughout such a long period of time. They have wisdom that has gone beyond doubt. This means they obtain the penetration of past lives. They know the things that happened in the past.

Q2 Separation from various destinies.

Sutra:

"**From that kalpa onward, through every life until the time they take their last body, they will not be born where there are yakshas, rakshasas, putanas, kataputanas, kumbhandas, pishachas and so forth; where there is any kind of hungry ghost, whether with form or lacking form, or with thought or lacking thought, or in any such evil place.**

Commentary:

From that kalpa onward, through every life until the time they take their last body, that is, when they become a Buddha, **they will not be born where there are yakshas.** They will be born and die again and again, but they will not be born in bad paths, such as that of the yakshas, "speedy ghosts." Nor will they be born where there are **rakshashas,** "terrifying ghosts" that eat people. When a person dies, this kind of ghost uses a mantra to change the flesh of the decaying corpse back into fresh meat and eats it. Nor will they have to be around **putanas,** "bad-smelling ghosts," which are both evil and foul-smelling. If you encounter such a ghost, you will contract a fever. "Putanas" are also known as "bhutanas." Nor will such people be born where there are **kataputanas,** "strange-smelling ghosts." The other one smelled bad, but this one smells weird – an odor you've never smelled before, one that is incredibly strong. That's what's referred to by the phrase: "It smelled so strange one could not bear to breathe." If you get a whiff of this odor, it will make you vomit on the spot. It connects with the bad-smelling stuff inside you, so that you have to regurgitate. You spit your insides out. It's that strong. This ghost causes fevers to an even greater degree of intensity. Your entire body burns with fevers up to 120 degrees and more; it simply burns your bones to ashes. Violent, wouldn't you say?

They won't be born where there are **kumbhandas**. Actually, all these ghosts have been mentioned before. The kumbhandas are "barrel-shaped ghosts." These ghosts paralyze people. They come on you in your sleep and paralyze you. You open your eyes to find that you can't move. Nor can you speak. At its fiercest, it can kill people with the paralysis. If a person has *yang* energy, then the paralysis won't hold. It only is effective on those who have excessive *yin* energy. What is meant by *yang*? It means always being happy, truly happy in your self-nature, that is, not just laughing it up on the surface of things, "ha, ha, ha." It refers to the extreme bliss experienced in your inherent nature. If in your self-nature you are always worried and depressed, being afflicted, upset, and distressed all day long, that belongs to *yin*. Those belonging to *yin* are the ones that ghosts can possess. *Yang* belongs to the spirit. Predominance of *yang* is a spirit; predominance of *yin* is a ghost. People who cultivate the Buddha path and have pure *yang* energy, also have light. But if one is totally *yin*, there is a black energy present. So, it can be told if a person is good or not just by looking at him or her. Good people have white energy around them; bad people have a mass of black energy, demonic energy.

They also will not be born where there are **pishachas and so forth.** Pishachas are "essence and energy-eating" ghosts. These ghosts sap the energy from things as well as from people. This kind of ghost is terrible and not at all good. For the most part, ghosts are bad, but among the path of ghosts are also bodhisattvas who compassionately and deliberately manifest as ghost-kings in order to take ghosts across.

Nor will they be born **where there is any kind of hungry ghost.** There are many types of hungry ghosts. Some have huge stomachs. Some have throats as skinny as needles. **Whether with form or lacking form.** Some have bodies, and some are invisible – they have no physical form. But, just because you can't see something, don't assume it isn't there. Invisible creatures may lack form, but they have consciousness. You cannot see them with the ordinary eyes but if you have the five eyes and six spiritual penetrations, it is easy to see them. **With thought or lacking thought.** Some have the capability of thought, while others have no thought; they are like dirt, wood, metal, and stone. But a person who upholds the Shurangama Mantra will not be born **in any such evil place.** Life after life, they will not be born in places where there are hungry ghosts or where there are any other kinds of evil.

Q3   Always born where there are Buddhas.

Sutra:

"**If these good people read, recite, copy, or write out the mantra, if they carry it or treasure it, if they make offerings to it, then through kalpa after kalpa they will not be poor or lowly, nor will they be born in unpleasant places.**

Commentary:

If these good people read the mantra from a book, or **recite** it from memory; if they **copy** it out respectfully, or casually **write it out; if they carry it** on their person, **or treasure it,** store it in their homes; **if they make offerings to it** of all kinds of incense and flowers, lamps, candles, and fruit – the Shurangama Mantra was spoken by a transformation body of the Buddha, so it is worthy of offerings – **then through kalpa after kalpa they will not be poor or lowly, nor will they be born in unpleasant places.** I've told you that if you can memorize the Shurangama Mantra to the point that it flows forth from your mind and heart, then you have obtained the samadhi of holding the mantra. Once you obtain that – if you can recite it like flowing water which never ceases – then at the very, very least, you can be fabulously wealthy for seven lives. If you continue reciting it in this way for life after life, you can be wealthy for seventy or seven hundred or seven thousand or seven million lives; there's nothing fixed about it. As long as you want to be a wealthy person, you can be one. But some day you may have had your fill, because even billionaires have their problems. You may get disgusted. Then you can become a Buddha. Once you become a Buddha, there are no more problems. At that point,

In a state of unmoving suchness,
You are ever bright and clear.

So, I'll give you a tip ahead of time. Being a billionaire is not as good as becoming a Buddha. People who uphold and venerate the mantra in these various ways will not be born in places that are worrisome and devoid of bliss. You could not go to those places even if you wanted to. Why? The Shurangama Mantra is pulling at you, telling you not to go. It will be impossible for you to go.

Sutra:

"**If these living beings have never accumulated any blessings, the Thus Come Ones of the ten directions will bestow their own merit and virtue upon these people.**

Commentary:

If these living beings who recite and uphold the Shurangama Mantra, **have never accumulated any blessings** – they've never done any good deeds or earned any blessings – then **the Thus Come Ones of the ten directions will bestow their own merit and virtue upon these people.** Why do they do that? Because these people recite the Shurangama Mantra, or read it, copy it, or write it out. They have no blessings, but the Buddhas of the ten directions give them blessings. A real bargain, wouldn't you say? All one must do is recite the Shurangama Mantra.

Sutra:

"**Because of that, throughout asamkhyeyas of ineffable, unspeakable numbers of kalpas, as many as the Ganges' sands, they are always together with the Buddhas. They are born in the same place, due to their limitless merit and virtue, and, like the amala fruit-cluster, they stay in the same place, become permeated with cultivation, and are never parted.**

Commentary:

Because of that, throughout asamkhyeyas of ineffable, unspeakable numbers of kalpas, as many as the Ganges' sands, they are always together with the Buddhas. "The Ganges' sands" indicates a large number. "Asamkhyeya" is also a large number; it means "limitless number" in Sanskrit. This refers to kalpas greater in number than could ever be expressed. **They are born in the same place, due to their limitless merit and virtue, and, like the amala fruit-cluster, they stay in the same place, become permeated with cultivation, and are never parted.** "Born in the same place" refers not so much to having the same birthplace, as to being born in the same generation. That is, they are always born at a time when there is a Buddha in the world. We are born at a time when there is no Buddha in the world. This is one of the eight difficulties: the difficulty of being born before or after the time of a Buddha. Those who are born when a Buddha is in the world are endowed with limitless merit and virtue. The amala fruit-cluster has three fruits on one stem. The fruits themselves are as if three and yet as if one. They cannot be separated one from the other. So, too, these people reside where the Buddha is and become infused with cultivation. They never have to be apart from the Buddha.

Q4 Various practices are accomplished.

Sutra:

"Therefore, it can enable those who have broken the precepts to regain the purity of the precept-source. It can enable those who have not received the precepts to receive them. It can cause those who are not vigorous to become vigorous. It can enable those who lack wisdom to gain wisdom. It can cause those who are not pure to quickly become pure. It can cause those who do not hold to vegetarianism to become vegetarians naturally.

Commentary:

Therefore, it can enable those who have broken the precepts to regain the purity of the precept-source. Even those who have broken the precepts can regain the precepts if they genuinely recite and uphold the Shurangama Mantra every day. Basically, someone who has violated the precepts cannot be saved, but if that person recites the Shurangama Mantra, it's possible for them to regain the purity of the precepts. Reciting doesn't just mean a casual recitation; you have to obtain the samadhi of holding mantras, as I just described. Then the mantra wells up from your heart and returns to your heart. That's what's meant by,

> The Mantra-heart,
> The Heart of the Mantra.
> The Heart of the Mantra,
> The Mantra-heart.

The mantra and your heart become one. There is no distinction between them. You cannot forget it; it recites itself. You are not reciting it, but it is being recited; you are reciting it, but it is as if you were not. Even if you don't want to recite it, it goes on being recited. Right now we recite the mantra before the sutra lecture, but that's just a way of preparing the ground for you. It's just pointing out the way for all of you. It's certainly not that it's only appropriate to recite the mantra at lecture time. You can recite it anywhere at any time. To know it by heart and to recite to the point that all other false thoughts and scattered thoughts are wiped away, and all that remains is your mind's recitation of the Shurangama Mantra: that's what is called concentration. The recitation comes together and there are no other thoughts. It's like flowing water that goes on and on, coming from afar and rolling by in wave after wave. It's like the blowing wind which comes up invisibly but makes its presence known.

> The water flows, the wind blows
> Proclaiming the Mahayana.

The sounds of the water and wind speak the great vehicle teachings; they are all the heart of the Shurangama Mantra.

When recitation reaches that state, **it can enable those who have broken the precepts to regain the purity of the precept source. It can cause those who have not received the precepts to obtain them. It can cause those who are not vigorous to become vigorous.** People who aren't inclined to progress, who don't investigate the Buddhadharma, can spontaneously give rise to vigor from reciting the Shurangama Mantra over a long period of time. **It can enable those who lack wisdom to gain wisdom.** Just look at this: it can enable stupid people to open their wisdom. **It can cause those who are not pure to quickly become pure.** If you cultivate and yet are not pure; if you violate the precepts, break the practice of pure eating, and get muddled and unclear for a long time; still, if you don't forget the Shurangama Mantra, you can quickly gain purity. Once you want to change, you can very quickly return to purity. For instance, I know there are those among you here who would like to study the Buddhadharma, but whose bodies and minds are not pure. But it doesn't matter if you lack purity; it's just to be feared you won't study. Because if you study, the day will come when you'll suddenly become pure. You will soon understand. But if you don't study, and you say, "I don't want to become pure; I don't want to be vigorous. I like being lazy. I'd rather not know anything" – then with that attitude there's nothing that can be done for you. **It can cause those who do not hold to vegetarianism to become vegetarians naturally.** If you recite the Shurangama Mantra until it comes together in a concentrated recitation, then the wind can't blow through and the rain can't penetrate. Then, even if you don't hold to vegetarianism, you will automatically do so. Why? Because you won't have any false thoughts, you won't have any greed or desires. You won't be thinking about wanting to eat meat or fish or delicious foods. It won't enter your mind.

Q5 All offenses are eradicated.

Sutra:

"Ananda, if good men who uphold this mantra violated the pure precepts before they received the mantra, their multitude of offenses incurred by violating the precepts, whether major or minor, can simultaneously be eradicated after they begin to uphold the mantra.

Commentary:

This passage gives a clearer explanation. **Ananda, if good men who uphold this mantra violated the pure precepts before they received the mantra** – if they uphold the mantra now, but violated the pure precepts in the past, breaking them before they received them, **their multitude of offenses incurred by violating the precepts, whether major or minor, can simultaneously be eradicated after they begin to uphold the mantra.** All their offenses of breaking the practice of pure eating and of violating the precepts can be eradicated, even the four parajika offenses – "parajika" means "cause for dismissal" meaning that they cannot be repented of. But if you recite the Shurangama Mantra, then all the offenses you have committed, no matter how serious, will be made clean; it is like pouring boiling water over snow.

Sutra:

"**Even if they drank intoxicants or ate the five pungent plants and various other impure things in the past, the Buddhas, bodhisattvas, vajras, gods, immortals, ghosts, and spirits will not hold it against them.**

Commentary:

The "five pungent plants" are leeks, garlic, shallots, scallions, and onions. These are the ones common to our area. *Asafoetida*, common in India and often found in curries is another pungent plant included in this list. Since these hot, pungent plants have unpleasant odors, they are prohibited in Buddhism for people who hold to pure eating practices. These are unclean kinds of things to eat and cause desire and anger. But, **even if they,** the holders of the mantra, **drank intoxicants or ate the five pungent plants and various other impure things** in the past, **the Buddhas, bodhisattvas, vajras, gods, immortals, ghosts, and spirits will not hold it against them.** If you can constantly recite and uphold the Shurangama Mantra, the Buddhas, bodhisattvas, and dharma protectors will not blame you for your former impure habits.

"If they won't hold it against me, then I can use these things as I please," you may reason. It's still best not to use them.

Sutra:

"If they are unclean and wear tattered, old clothes to carry out the single practice and single dwelling, they can be equally pure. Even if they do not set up the platform, do not enter the bodhimanda, and do not practice the Way, but recite and uphold this mantra, their merit and virtue will be identical with that derived from entering the platform and practicing the Way.

Commentary:

If they are unclean and wear tattered, old clothes to carry out the single practice and single dwelling – above, when the platform was described, the Buddha said that one should put on new clothes, but here he says one doesn't necessarily have to wear new clothes. If you don't have new clothes, old ones will do. When you go through the three weeks of practice, you can become pure just the same. Because of the power of the mantra, it makes no difference if the clothes you wear are new or old. The purity obtained is the same. You may wonder why he said to wear new clothes in the first place. We wear new clothes to signify our respect – out of utmost reverence and absolute purity. **Even if they do not set up the platform, do not enter the bodhimanda** – you don't necessarily have to be inside the bodhimanda. Any place at any time is a place of practice. If they **do not practice the Way** – even if they don't cultivate – **but recite and uphold this mantra** – that's all they are able to do in the way of practice – **their merit and virtue will be identical with that derived from entering the platform and practicing the Way.** If you can recite the Shurangama Mantra, your merit and virtue are no different from one who can set up the platform and enter the bodhimanda to practice the Way. There is no distinction. Truly, the virtue of the Shurangama Mantra is inconceivable!

Sutra:

"If they have committed the five rebellious acts, grave offenses warranting unintermittent retribution, or if they are bhikshus or bhikshunis who have violated the four parajikas or the eight parajikas, such heavy karma as this will disperse after they recite this mantra, like a sand dune that is scattered in a gale, so that not a particle remains."

Commentary:

If they have committed the five rebellious acts, grave offenses warranting unintermittent retribution – the five rebellious acts are the most serious offenses in all of Buddhism. They are:

1. killing one's mother;
2. killing one's father;
3. killing an arhat;
4. causing schisms in the harmonious Sangha;
5. shedding the Buddha's blood.

If you deliberately injure the Buddha's body with a knife or some such weapon, or if in some other way you draw blood on the Buddha's body, you have committed this offense.

"I've never even encountered a Buddha. The Buddha left the world, so I have no chance of committing this offense," you say.

Not so, because to deface a Buddha image or break it is also called shedding the Buddha's blood. Even prints and paintings of Buddhas are included in this. To destroy images of the Buddha when he is not in the world is also included in this offense. "Uninterrupted retribution" refers to the consequence of these offenses. Committing the ten evils brings a bad retribution, but committing the five rebellious acts results in a more severe punishment. If you commit the five rebellious acts, you will certainly fall into the Relentless Hell. This hell has been described before. It's full, whether there is one person in it or many people in it. Therefore, it is also called "unspaced," since there is no space in it. It's called unintermittent because the suffering never slacks off even for a second nor does it ever end. It goes on interminably.

If they are bhikshus or bhikshunis who have violated the four parajikas or the eight parajikas. "Bhikshu" has three meanings:

1. mendicant;
2. frightener of Mara;
3. destroyer of evil.

A "bhikshuni" is a female member of the Sangha. The four parajikas are:

1. sexual misconduct;
2. killing;
3. stealing;
4. making false claims.

These are the four fundamental precepts – "parajikas" in Sanskrit, "causes for dismissal" in English. If you commit any of these four, then you are dismissed from the Sangha of Buddhism. You are cast out of the great sea of the Buddhadharma. And you cannot re-enter. The four parajikas are for bhikshus. Bhikshunis have eight parajikas. They include the four for the bhikshus, plus:

5. touching;
6. the eight things;
7. covering;
8. not following.

The parajika offense of "touching" is described in the vinaya as "making contact with a woman while harboring thoughts of sexual desire." So whether it be a man, a woman, a bhikshu, or a bhikshuni, or a layperson, physical contact between people when there are thoughts of sexual desire is a violation. If one does not have thoughts of sexual desire, there is no violation of the precepts.

The parajika of "the eight things." A bhikshuni must always be in an open public place when she converses. She cannot go to a concealed place to talk or in a room where she would be alone with a man. In general, a man and woman cannot be alone together – be they bhikshuni or bhikshu. For a bhikshu this is a lighter offense; for a bhikshuni it is a heavy one. It is forbidden that a bhikshuni talk alone with a man.

"Covering" means concealing another's offenses. You hide someone else's grave offenses and are not frank and open about them. You don't tell anyone. That's also a parajika offense for bhikshunis.

"Not following" refers to the recitation of precepts which takes place twice a month on the first and fifteenth of the lunar calendar. When bhikshus are present in a place where bhikshunis are, the bhikshunis must follow along with the recitation of the precepts by the bhikshus. They cannot recite the precepts themselves and take personal offerings. If they don't accord with this method, they violate this precept of not following. These are the eight parajikas for bhikshunis.

But even for people who have committed such serious violations, **such heavy karma as this will disperse after they recite this mantra like a sand dune that is scattered in a gale, so that not a particle remains.** Even the five rebellious acts and the four and eight parajikas can be blown away by the recitation of the mantra, just as a strong wind blows away a sand dune so that it totally disappears. Not a hair's breadth of offense remains. This again shows the inconceivable power of the Shurangama Mantra.

Q6　Quick certification to non-production.

Sutra:

"Ananda, if living beings who have never repented and reformed any of the obstructive offenses, either heavy or light, that they have committed throughout countless kalpas past, up to and including those of this very life, can nevertheless read, recite, copy, or write out this mantra or wear it on their bodies

or place it in their homes or in their garden houses, then all that accumulated karma will melt away like snow in hot water. Before long they will obtain awakening to patience with the non-existence of beings and phenomena.

Commentary:

Ananda, if living beings who have never repented and reformed any of the obstructive offenses, either heavy or light, that they have committed throughout countless kalpas past, up to and including those of this very life. They have never had an opportunity to repent of them and reform. "Repent" means to be sorry about one's former offenses. "Reform" means to change so one does not commit the errors again. They **can nevertheless read** the Shurangama Mantra, or **recite** it, **copy** it out, **or write** it **out**. Reciting of the mantra must be done over a long term. The Buddha isn't talking about reciting it once or twice. He means over and over for a very long time. **Or** they **wear it on their bodies.** When you carry the mantra on your body, you want to wear it above your heart, not below. To wear it above your heart represents respect; if you carry it on the lower part of your body, you are not showing proper respect for the mantra. Not only is there no merit in that, you are actually committing offenses. If you are not respectful to the mantra itself, then the efficacy of the mantra is depleted with regard to you. **Or** they **place it in their homes or in their garden houses. Then all that accumulated karma** from the offenses committed in life after life, as mentioned above, **will melt away like snow in hot water.** The offenses will disappear just that quickly. **Before long they will attain awakening to patience with the non-existence of beings and phenomena.**

P3   Answers all kinds of wishes.

Sutra:

"**Moreover, Ananda, if women who do not have children and want to conceive can sincerely memorize and recite this mantra or carry the mantra, Syi Dan Dwo Bwo Da La, on their bodies,**

they can give birth to sons or daughters endowed with blessings, virtue, and wisdom.

Commentary:

"Moreover, Ananda," the Buddha continues, **"if women who do not have children and want to conceive"** – suppose there are women who would like to be mothers. They would like to get pregnant. If they **can sincerely memorize and recite this mantra or carry the mantra, Syi Dan Dwo Bwo Da La, on their bodies, they can give birth to sons or daughters endowed with blessings, virtue, and wisdom.** "Sincerely" means single-mindedly; it means to reach the ultimate point of sincere regard. Perhaps they can remember it or use the book to recite the Shurangama Mantra. Or perhaps they request a high master endowed with virtue in the Way to copy out for them the heart of the mantra, **Syi Dan Dwo Bwo Da La,** and they carry that on their bodies. This phrase of the mantra means a great white canopy, whether you wear the syllables on your person or are mindful of them in your mind, a great, white canopy spreads out in the air above you and protects you. It can fulfill all your wishes. If these women do these things, their wishes can be fulfilled, and quite soon in response to their sincerity they will have children with blessings, virtue, and wisdom. If they want sons, they will get sons; if they want daughters, they will get daughters.

Sutra:

"Those who seek long life will obtain long life. Those who seek to quickly perfect their reward will quickly gain perfection. The same is true for those who seek something regarding their bodies, their lives, their appearance, or their strength.

Commentary:

Those who recite the Shurangama Mantra and **seek long life will obtain long life.** They will get that reward. **Those who seek to quickly perfect their reward,** whatever good reward it might be they want, **will quickly gain perfection.** For instance, if a woman hopes to have a good husband in the future, that's a kind of good reward. And she can attain it. The same applies to men. The meaning is that whatever you seek you can have. It is said,

> Those who seek wealth and honor,
> get wealth and honor.
> Those who seek long life,
> obtain long life.
> Those who seek sons,
> get sons;
> Those who seek daughters,
> get daughters.

No matter what it is, you can have your wishes fulfilled and have everything be as you would like it. **The same is true for those who seek something regarding their bodies, their lives, their appearances, or their strength.** Whatever they seek on behalf of these things, they will obtain it, in the same way one seeks and obtains long life, and the like.

Sutra:

"At the end of their lives, they will gain the rebirth they hope for in whichever of the countries of the ten directions they wish. They certainly will not be born in poorly endowed places, or as inferior people; even less will they be reborn in some odd form.

Commentary:

At the end of their lives, they will gain the rebirth they hope for in whichever of the countries of the ten directions they wish. If you want to be reborn in the East, and come before Akshobhya Buddha, or in the West and meet Amitabha Buddha, or in the North, or in the South – it's up to you – you can be reborn in the country of whichever Buddha you would like to draw near to. **They certainly will not be born in poorly endowed places, or as inferior people.** "Poorly endowed" refers to places where the land is not rich and the people are not educated. If one can recite the

Shurangama Mantra, one will not be born in such places; **even less will they be reborn in some odd form.** As a person, you will not have an inferior rebirth; even less will you be reborn as an animal.

O2 Apparent universal benefit to the land.
P1 All difficulties disappear.

Sutra:

"Ananda, if there is famine or plague in a country, province, or village, or if perhaps there are armed troops, brigands, invasions, war, or any other kind of local threat or danger, one can write out this spiritual mantra and place it on the four city gates, or on a chaitya or on a dhvaja, and instruct all the people of the country to gaze upon the mantra, to make obeisance to it, to revere it, and to single-mindedly make offerings to it; one can instruct all the citizens to wear it on their bodies or to place it in their homes; and then all such disasters and calamities will completely disappear.

Commentary:

Ananda, if there is famine or plague in a country, province, or village – this means any country at all, whether as large as an entire continent, or as small as a local area or village. In time of famine, there may have been drought, so that nothing will grow, or at the other extreme there may have been a torrential rain which drowns the crops. When a plague strikes, a violent contagious disease spreads among the population and is fatal if contracted. **Or if perhaps there are armed troops, brigands, invasions, war, or any other kind of local threat or danger** – in any of these places where there are such difficulties – **one can write out this spiritual mantra and place it on the four city gates, or on a chaitya.** They can place it on the archway above the gates. "Chaitya" is a Sanskrit word for pagoda, a place which houses the relics of a Buddha or sage. **Or,** they can place it **on a dhvaja.** "Dhvaja" is a Sanskrit word for "banner." Perhaps the mantra is written on a flag and flown high above the city from a watchtower or flagpole. **And** one **instructs all the people of the country to gaze upon the mantra,**

to make obeisance to it, to revere it, and to single-mindedly make offerings to it. One can instruct all the citizens of the country to wear it on their bodies or to place it in their homes. People can carry the mantra on themselves or put a copy of it in the places where they live, and then all such disasters and calamities will completely disappear. All these misfortunes and evil events will be done away with. The merit and virtue of the Shurangama Mantra is inconceivable. You can't imagine it or think about it; that's where the wonder of it lies.

Some people think that cultivation can consist of nothing but meditation, and so they don't study the sutras. But that is a mistake. Others may think merely reciting mantras and studying the sutras will work and that they don't need to meditate. That's also not the right way. Some may hear how efficacious and powerful mantras are, so they merely recite mantras and do not cultivate in other ways. This is also behavior that is too extreme. In cultivation, no matter what method you cultivate, you must find the Middle Way. Don't get carried away. On the other hand, don't fail to go far enough. Too much is the same as not enough. True enough, mantras are efficacious, but you must also develop your samadhi power. This sutra stresses that the mantra is efficacious, but the most essential point as far as cultivation is concerned is its teaching of the dharma door of turning the hearing back to hear the self-nature – the dharma door of the perfect penetration of the organ of the ear. So even when you recite mantras, you should be turning the hearing back to hear the self nature. You should return the light and illumine within.

When you recite the mantra, the mantra is one's mind and one's mind is the mantra. The two cannot be separated. The mind and the mantra are two and yet not two. Although they are two, they become one. If you can become like that, then whatever you want will be as you wish. You will certainly be able to accomplish what you set out to do. If the mantra and your mind unite as one, then you will obtain the samadhi of Chan. This is something that everyone should be aware of.

P2 The people experience plenty and happiness.

Sutra:

"Ananda, in each and every country where the people accord with this mantra, the heavenly dragons are delighted, the winds and rains are seasonal, the crops are abundant, and the people are peaceful and happy.

Commentary:

Ananda, in each and every country where the people accord with this mantra, the heavenly dragons are delighted. No matter what country it may be, if the Shurangama Mantra is there, the heavenly dragons are pleased, and **the winds and rains are seasonal.** There are no hurricanes or floods which bring harm and destruction. **The crops are abundant.** There are plentiful harvests of the five grains. **The people are peaceful and happy.**

P3 Evil omens do not manifest.

Sutra:

"It can also suppress all evil stars which may appear in any of the directions and transform themselves in uncanny ways. Calamities and obstructions will not arise. People will not die accidentally or unexpectedly, nor will they be bound by fetters, cangues, or locks. Day and night they will be at peace, and no evil dreams will disturb their sleep.

Commentary:

This passage tells how they will not have the difficulty of evil dreams, either. **It also can suppress all evil stars.** The mantra can control the influence of ill-omened stars. This is just like a person of genuine wisdom ruling a country in such a way that there are no rebels; all the bad people reform, and all matters are conducted with ease. When one person endowed with virtue in the Way is the leader, an entire country of people of lesser endowment will willingly follow. They will heed his wisdom. Here, the mantra is analogous to the virtuous leader. It can control all inauspicious events. The "evil stars" represent unlucky affairs. These bad stars

may appear in any of the directions and transform themselves in uncanny ways. They can bring about terrible, cruel disasters. But **calamities and obstructions will not arise. People will not die accidentally or unexpectedly.** "Accidental" deaths are untimely, unlucky deaths such as fatal auto accidents, or airplane crashes, or drowning at sea, or deaths by burning. The passage refers to anything that causes people to die when they don't want to, when they aren't prepared. "Unexpected deaths" refers to the death of children. Any death before one is thirty years old is considered unexpected, because one has not lived out one's proper lifespan. **Nor will they be bound by fetters, cangues, or locks. Day and night they will be at peace, and no evil dreams will disturb their sleep.** No ghosts will come to bully you.

Sutra:

"**Ananda, this Saha world has eighty-four thousand changeable and disastrous evil stars. Twenty-eight great evil stars are the leaders, and of these, eight great evil stars are the rulers. They take various shapes, and when they appear in the world they bring disaster and weird happenings upon living beings.**

Commentary:

Ananda, this Saha world has eighty-four thousand changeable and disastrous evil stars. There are uncountably many evil stars connected with this world we live in. **Twenty-eight great evil stars are the leaders.** Although these twenty-eight are evil, they can also be good. In China, twenty-eight constellations which rule the four directions are spoken of, with seven constellations in each direction. In Chinese astrology, these constellations rule all divisions of time, even down to the days and hours. One cycle takes twenty-eight days, the typical lunar month. If a person is good, then the evil stars change to good ones. If the people of a certain place are evil, however, then even the good stars can change to evil ones. So it's not that the stars are inherently evil or good; it's that they respond to the influence of karmic retribution and manifest in good or evil ways. Here they are referred to as evil to show that the Shurangama Mantra can dissolve all calamities and difficulties. Thus, the sutra takes the position at this point that all the stars are evil – that all are inauspicious. If the stars are inauspicious and you as a person don't have any great good roots or any virtuous conduct to your benefit, then of course the whole situation becomes even more inauspicious. But if you can recite the Shurangama Mantra, then even inauspicious events can change to auspicious ones.

The twenty-eight are:

二十八宮

Thursday	Friday	Saturday	Sunday	Monday	Tuesday	Wednesday
1 角 jue	2 亢 kang	3 氐 di	4 房 fang	5 心 xin	6 尾 wei	7 箕 ji
8 斗 dou	9 牛 niu	10 女 nu	11 虛 xu	12 危 wei	13 室 shi	14 壁 bi
15 奎 kui	16 婁 lou	17 胃 wei	18 昴 mao	19 畢 bi	20 觜 zui	21 參 shen
22 井 jing	23 鬼 gui	24 柳 lu	25 星 xing	26 張 zhang	27 翼 yi	28 軫 zhen

And of these, eight great evil stars are the rulers:
1. "Wood Star," Jupiter
2. "Fire Star," Mars
3. "Earth Star," Saturn
4. "Metal Star," Venus
5. "Water Star," Mercury
6. Rahu (North Node)
7. Ketu (South Node)
8. Comets

Some celestial bodies are terrible and ugly; some are elegant and beautiful to behold. During the change of dynasties in China, a comet appeared in the world. Actually, what was the comet? It was a child wearing a red nightshirt. It went about teaching children to sing. When all the children started singing, the country would come to an end. So it was that whenever the government was about to change hands and a new emperor was about to appear, this evil star would appear in the world. "Weird happenings" refers to things not ordinarily seen. Suddenly some special circumstance arises that is totally out of the ordinary, and always inauspicious. "Happenings" means that things would change and be out of balance and not proper.

Sutra:

"But they will all be eradicated wherever there is the mantra. The boundaries will be secured for twelve yojanas around, and no evil calamity or misfortune will ever enter in.

Commentary:

But they will all be eradicated – all inauspicious events, calamities, and disasters – **wherever there is the mantra** – in every country where the Shurangama Mantra is known. **The boundaries will be secured for twelve yojanas around.** One secures the boundaries by reciting the mantra in a certain place. For instance, one recites the Shurangama Mantra while facing north, then east, then south, then west. In every direction that one faces while reciting, the boundaries are secured for a distance of twelve *yojanas*. A small yojana is forty Chinese miles (about thirteen English miles). "Twelve yojanas" here refers to great yojanas, or a total of ninety-six Chinese miles (thirty-two English miles). For that distance all around, the boundaries are secured. Within that range, the demons and weird creatures and ghosts are not permitted to cause accidents or catastrophies. They are not permitted to act up and make trouble. Beyond the thirty-six miles it is a different matter, but within them, **no evil calamity or misfortune will ever enter in.** Thus, wherever the Shurangama Mantra is found, everyone in the area benefits. In the area where the boundaries are secured, no catastrophe, calamity, accident, or misfortune will be found.

M3 He makes clear with a general exhortation that cultivators will certainly certify.
N1 They will be protected and peaceful.

Sutra:

"Therefore, the Thus Come One proclaims this mantra as one which will protect those of the future who have just begun to study, as well as all cultivators, so that they can enter samadhi, be peaceful in body and mind, and attain great tranquility.

Commentary:

Therefore, the Thus Come One, Shakyamuni Buddha, **proclaims** the Shurangama Mantra as the mantra **which will protect those of the future.** That refers to us in the present. He says that this mantra will protect those in the future **who have just begun to study, as well as all cultivators so that they can enter samadhi.** They will obtain samadhi power, **be peaceful in body and mind, and attain great tranquillity.** They will be calm and free from troubles.

N2 They will be far apart from demons and enemies.

Sutra:

"Even less will any demon, ghost, or spirit, or any enemy, calamity, or misfortune due from former lives that reach back to beginningless time, or any old karma or past debts come to vex and harm them.

Commentary:

Even less will any demon, ghost, or spirit, or any enemy, calamity, or misfortune due from former lives that reach back to beginningless time come to bother one who holds this mantra. Misfortunes due from a former life refer to offenses one created for which one should undergo a retribution. This also is true for **any old karma**, that is, for deeds done in former lives – karmic obstacles one has created **or past debts** one owes. For instance, if one has killed a person, one should have to pay back with one's own life. If one eats another's flesh, one has to pay back with one's own flesh. All these debts have to be paid off. But if one can recite and uphold the Shurangama Mantra, these misfortunes due from old karma and past unpaid debts will not **come to vex and harm** one. Nothing can get at you.

N3 They will not commit four violations.
N4 They must keep their minds on their recitation.

Sutra:

"**As to you and everyone in the assembly who is still studying, and as to cultivators of the future who rely on my platform, hold the precepts in accord with the dharma, receive the precepts from pure members of the Sangha, and hold this mantra-heart without giving rise to doubts: should such good people as these not obtain mind-penetration in that very body born of their parents, then the Thus Come Ones of the ten directions have lied!**"

Commentary:

As to you, Ananda, **and everyone in the assembly who is still studying, and as to cultivators of the future.** That includes all of us of the present time. If all of these **rely on my platform** – if they establish platforms in accord with the method I have described – **and hold the precepts in accord with the dharma**; if they **receive the precepts from pure members of the Sangha** – they meet members of the Sangha who are pure and who have not violated the precepts; and if they **hold this mantra-heart without giving rise to doubts** – they do not have even the slightest doubt about the Shurangama Mantra: **should such good people as these** rely on my method to cultivate, establish the platform, and meet a pure bhikshu from whom they receive the complete precepts – if such are their causes and conditions; then if **in that very body born of their parents**, they do **not obtain the mind-penetration** – that is, if they don't become enlightened and obtain the five eyes and six spiritual penetrations – **then the Thus Come Ones of the ten directions have lied!** Then the Buddhas of the ten directions are not telling the truth.

I3 The assembly vows to protect it.
J1 The outer assembly protects and holds it.
K1 The multitude of vajra power-knights.

Sutra:

When he finished this explanation, measureless hundreds of thousands of vajra power-knights in the assembly came before the Buddha, placed their palms together, bowed, and said, "With sincere hearts we will protect those who cultivate bodhi in this way, according to what the Buddha has said."

Commentary:

When he, Shakyamuni Buddha, **finished this explanation, measureless hundreds of thousands of vajra power-knights in the assembly came before the Buddha, placed their palms together, bowed, and said** to the Buddha, **"With sincere hearts we will protect those who cultivate bodhi in this way, according to what the Buddha has said**, according to this dharma-door. We will guard all the sincere good people who are cultivating like this to attain the bodhi way."

K2 The venerable hosts of gods.

Sutra:

Then the Brahma king, the god Shakra, and the four great heavenly kings all came before the Buddha, made obeisance together, and said to the Buddha, "If indeed there be good men who cultivate and study in this way, we will do all we can to earnestly protect them and cause everything to be as they would wish throughout their entire lives."

Commentary:

Then the Brahma king, the lord of the Great Brahma Heaven, **the god Shakra,** Lord God, **and the four great heavenly kings** also **came before the Buddha.** They all stood up together and then **made obeisance together** to the Buddha, **and said to the Buddha, "If indeed there be good men who cultivate and study in this way, we will do all we can to earnestly protect them and cause**

everything to be as they would wish throughout their entire lives. If there really are people who cultivate as you have described just now, Buddha, then with the fullest measure of our sincerity, we will guard and protect them and fulfill their wishes."

K3   The host of the eight divisions.

Sutra:

Moreover, measureless great yaksha generals, rakshasa kings, putana kings, kumbhanda kings, pishacha kings, Vinayaka, the great ghost kings, and all the ghost commanders came before the Buddha, put their palms together, and made obeisance. "We also have vowed to protect these people and cause their resolve for bodhi to be quickly perfected."

Commentary:

Moreover, measureless great yaksha generals, the "speedy" ghosts; **rakshasa kings,** the "terrifying" ghosts which are full of devious tricks; **putana kings,** the "bad-smelling" ghosts which cause fevers; **kumbhanda kings,** the "barrel-shaped" ghosts which paralyze people; **pishacha** are another horrible kind of ghost; **Vinayaka,** the scary, ugly dharma protector; **the great ghost kings; and all the ghost commanders came before the Buddha, put their palms together, made obeisance** together, and said to the Buddha, **"We also have vowed to protect these people and cause their resolve for bodhi to be quickly perfected."**

K4   The ruling assembly of illumining bodies.

Sutra:

Further, measureless numbers of gods of the sun and moon, lords of the rain, lords of the clouds, lords of thunder, lords of lightning who patrol throughout the year, and all the retinues of stars which were also in the assembly bowed at the Buddha's feet and said to the Buddha, "We also protect all cultivators, so that their bodhimandas are peaceful and they attain fearlessness."

Commentary:

  Further, measureless numbers of gods of the sun and moon, lords of the rain, lords of the clouds, lords of thunder, lords of lightning who patrol throughout the year – most people don't realize that for every year there is a governor who monitors the events that take place during it – **and all the retinues of stars which were also in the assembly** – each star has its retinue – **bowed at the Buddha's feet and said to the Buddha, "We also protect all cultivators, so that their bodhimandas are peaceful and they attain fearlessness.** We've also made vows to protect people who cultivate. We set ourselves up in their bodhimanda and help them be unafraid. They attain the power of fearlessness."

K5   The deities and spirits of the earth.

Sutra:

  Moreover, measureless numbers of mountain spirits, sea spirits, and all those of the earth – the myriad creatures and essences of water, land, and the air – as well as the king of wind spirits and the gods of the formless heavens, came before the Thus Come One, bowed their heads, and said to the Buddha, "We also will protect these cultivators until they attain bodhi and will never let any demons have their way with them."

Commentary:

  Moreover, measureless numbers of mountain spirits, sea spirits, and all those of the earth – the myriad creatures and essences of water, land, and the air – all these spirits, too – **as well as the king of the wind spirits and the gods of the formless heavens, came before the Thus Come One, bowed their heads,** simultaneously making obeisance to the Buddha, **and said to the Buddha, "We also will protect these cultivators until they attain bodhi and will never let any demons have their way with them.** We will protect them right up to the time they attain bodhi and will never let anything demonic happen to them."

J2	The inner sages protect and hold it.
K1	They reveal their origin and their long-term protection.

Sutra:

Then Vajra-Treasury-King Bodhisattvas in the great assembly, numbering as many as eighty-four thousand nayutas of kotis' worth of sands in the Ganges, arose from their seats, bowed at the Buddha's feet, and said to the Buddha, "World Honored One, the nature of our deeds in cultivation is such that, although we have long since accomplished bodhi, we do not grasp at nirvana, but always accompany those who hold this mantra, rescuing and protecting those in the final age who cultivate samadhi properly.

Commentary:

Then Vajra-Treasury-King Bodhisattvas in the great assembly, numbering as many as eighty-four thousand nayutas of kotis – that is, as many hundreds of millions – **worth of sands in the Ganges, arose from their seats, bowed at the Buddha's feet, and said to the Buddha, "World Honored One, the nature of our deeds in cultivation is such that, although we have long since accomplished bodhi, we do not grasp at nirvana, but always accompany those who hold this mantra.** The merit and virtue of our cultivation is such that we already realized bodhi long ago; we have been certified. So why don't we enter nirvana? We always accompany those who hold this mantra. We are intent upon **rescuing and protecting those in the final age who cultivate samadhi properly.** Those who genuinely practice Chan samadhi will be guarded and protected by us."

K2	They assert their protection and maintaining.

Sutra:

"World Honored One, such people as this, who cultivate their minds and seek proper concentration, whether in the bodhimanda or walking about, and even such people who with

scattered minds roam and play in the villages, will be accompanied and protected by us and our retinue of followers.

Commentary:

The Vajra-Treasury-King Bodhisattvas continue speaking to the Buddha: **World Honored One, such people as this, who cultivate their minds and seek proper concentration** – who want to obtain genuine samadhi power – **whether in the bodhimanda or walking about.** Cultivators sit in meditation and apply effort, but when they get up and walk about, they are still applying effort. When they sit, they develop the skill of dhyana samadhi. When they get up, they cultivate the samadhi of reciting and holding, either by reciting mantras or being mindful of the Buddha. **And even such people who with scattered minds roam and play in the villages.** The Vajra-Treasury-King Bodhisattvas even protect cultivators who are not cultivating samadhi, are not in the bodhimanda, and are not walking about reciting. Actually, though, even if you're on a holiday to another place, you can still hold the mantra. But even if you get scattered, the Vajra Treasury-King Bodhisattvas say: you **will be accompanied and protected by us and our retinue of followers.** If you are one who recites and upholds the Shurangama Mantra, and if you have some skill, if you can make it function, then eighty-four thousand Vajra-Treasury-King Bodhisattvas and their entire retinue of followers will accompany and protect you wherever you go, just as troops protect their generals. When you enter a room, there will be guards at the door protecting you.

Sutra:

"Although the demon kings and the god of great comfort will seek to get at them, they will never be able to do so. The smaller ghosts will have to stay ten yojanas' distance from these good people, except for those beings who have decided they want to cultivate dhyana.

Commentary:

Although the demon kings and the god of great comfort will seek to get at them, they will never be able to do so. They will look for a way in, they will look for a hole, so that they can give the cultivators trouble. But they will not be able to bother them. And **the smaller ghosts will have to stay ten yojanas' distance from these good people.** Since the demon kings and the god of the Heaven of Great Comfort are unable to disturb them, the little ghosts and spirits will have to behave even more properly. They will have to stay 275 miles away, **except for those beings who have decided they want to cultivate dhyana.** The only exception is those ghosts who have brought forth the resolve to listen to the sutras, hear the dharma, and to cultivate Chan samadhi. Beings like that can participate in the bodhimanda and the dharma assemblies and can listen to the sutras if they want to. If they don't want to do those things, they must stay 275 miles away.

Sutra:

"**World Honored One, if such evil demons or their retinues want to harm or disturb these good people, we will smash their heads to smithereens with our vajra pestles. We will always help these people to accomplish what they want.**"

Commentary:

Would you say the dharma-protecting Vajra-Treasury Bodhisattvas are fierce? They say they will smash the heads of demons into fine motes of dust. Can you imagine how much strength that would take? I'll tell you, however, that there is no need for the vajra pestles of the Vajra-Treasury Bodhisattvas to come in actual contact with the heads of the demons at all. They don't need to really strike a blow in order to smash their heads to smithereens. All they have to do is have the thought to do it, and the deed is accomplished. That's because the strength of the samadhi of the Vajra-Treasury Bodhisattvas is sufficient to obliterate everything that exists. So they call out again: **World Honored One, if such evil demons or their retinues want to harm or disturb these good people, we will smash their heads to smithereens with our vajra pestles. We will always help these people to accomplish what they want.** Just such demons as those mentioned here are behind the brawls and strikes and revolts, the cases of arson, murder, and theft in every major city in the world today. Demon kings stir up these troubles invisibly. Most people don't know that but someone who has cultivated the Buddhadharma to the point that he or she has genuine samadhi power – someone with good roots who has opened the buddha eye – can verify that this is so. The problem is that the devious devices of the demons have a lot of power behind them. They pack more of a wallop than the Buddhadharma, in that one must cultivate the dharma for a long, long time – three, five, ten, twenty years – before one obtains a little advantage. But the demons' tricks are mastered very swiftly. They can cultivate and obtain tremendous psychic powers, and they abound throughout the world, causing unrest and instigating trouble. However, if you can recite the Shurangama Mantra, then all the demons throughout the world are forced to behave to some extent. If no one can recite the Shurangama Mantra, they will run rampant. They will recklessly devastate this world.

CHAPTER 4

The Two Upside-down Causes

F4 He explains certification to the position of dhyana causing him to dwell in complete samadhi and tend straight toward bodhi.
G1 Ananda is grateful for the instruction and asks about the position.

Sutra:

Then Ananda arose from his seat, bowed at the Buddha's feet, and said to the Buddha, "Now that we who are stupid and slow, who are fond of erudition but have not sought to cease the outflows of our minds, have received the Buddha's compassionate instructions and have attained the proper means to become infused with cultivation, we experience joy in body and mind and obtain tremendous benefit.

Commentary:

Then Ananda arose from his seat, bowed at the Buddha's feet, and said to the Buddha: Now that we who are stupid and slow, that is, those of us in the assembly who still must study and must rely on our memories, **who are fond of erudition but have not sought to cease the outflows of our minds**: we like to read, to study, and to memorize. We are quite clever at that. But as to the outflows of our thoughts and actions, we have not sought to get rid of them. We have not decided we want to transcend the triple realm. We are not concerned about getting out of the burning house. Now that we **have received the Buddha's compassionate instructions and have attained the proper means to become infused with cultivation, we experience joy in body and mind and obtain tremendous benefit.** The Buddha has now taught us the genuine methods that we should cultivate and steep ourselves in. This makes us very happy. It's been of great benefit to us.

Sutra:

"**World Honored One, for one who cultivates in this way and is certified as having attained the Buddha's samadhi, but who has not yet reached nirvana, what is meant by the level of dry wisdom? What are the forty-four minds? What is the sequence in which one cultivates till one reaches one's goal? What place must one reach to be said to have entered the grounds? And what is meant by a bodhisattva of equal enlightenment?**"

Commentary:

World Honored One, for one who cultivates in this way and is certified as having attained the Buddha's samadhi, but who has not yet reached nirvana, what is meant by the level of dry wisdom? Buddha, we cultivate in this way until we are certified to the fruition and give proof to the Buddha's samadhi power. But before we reach nirvana, there are many levels to pass through. What is the level of dry wisdom, for example? **What are the forty-four minds? What is the sequence in which one cultivates till one reaches one's goal? What place must one reach to be said to have entered the grounds?** How do we know when we reach the level of the tenth ground bodhisattva? **And what is meant by a bodhisattva of equal enlightenment?** Since all these terms are going to be explained in the subsequent passages, we will not go into them here.

Sutra:

Having said this, he made a full prostration, and then the great assembly single-mindedly awaited the sound of the

Buddha's compassionate voice as they gazed up unblinking with respectful admiration.

Commentary:

After Ananda had **said this, he made a full prostration.** He and everyone in the great assembly placed their five limbs – their head, arms, and legs – on the ground in full obeisance. **And then the great assembly single-mindedly awaited the sound of the Buddha's compassionate voice as they gazed up unblinking with respectful admiration.** They gazed with such fixed intensity that it was as if they could not see. They waited expectantly for the Buddha to speak. What do you suppose the Buddha is going to say?

G2 The Thus Come One answers with instruction in the arisal of conditions.
H1 The Thus Come One offers to speak and the great assembly waits to hear.

Sutra:

At that time the World Honored One praised Ananda, saying, "Good indeed, good indeed, that you can for the sake of the entire great assembly and those beings in the final age who cultivate samadhi and seek the great vehicle, ask to have explained and revealed the unsurpassed proper path of cultivation that takes one from the level of an ordinary person to final parinirvana. Listen attentively, and I will speak about it for you." Ananda and everyone in the assembly placed their palms together, cleansed their minds, and silently waited to receive the teaching.

Commentary:

At that time refers to the period when the great assembly was gazing up unblinkingly with respectful admiration. **The World Honored One praised Ananda.** He perceived how sincere Ananda and the great assembly were, so he praised him by saying: **Good indeed, good indeed,** you are certainly a good person. **You can for the sake of the entire great assembly and those beings of the final age.** It is excellent that you who still have something left to study can seek for the sake of everyone and not just for yourselves. You are not being selfish or seeking self-benefit in doing this. You are doing it for everyone assembled here and also for beings to come in the future who cultivate samadhi and who want to practice the great vehicle practices of benefiting themselves and benefiting others, and so you **ask to have explained and revealed the unsurpassed proper path of cultivation that takes one from the level of an ordinary person to final parinirvana.** Nirvana is the fruition where there is neither production nor extinction. You haven't arrived at it yet, but you wish to know about the proper way to get there. **Listen attentively, and I will speak about it for you.** Pay close attention. I am willing to explain it for you.

Ananda and everyone in the assembly placed their palms together, cleansed their minds, and silently waited to receive the teaching. "Cleansed their minds" means that they cast out their extraneous thoughts, the false thinking of their conscious mind – their mad mind and wild nature. They got rid of the five quick causes,

1. the point of view of a body,
2. prejudiced views,
3. the point of view of unbeneficial precepts,
4. opinionated views, and
5. deviant views,

as well as the five slow causes,

1. greed,
2. hatred,
3. stupidity,
4. pride, and
5. doubt.

Just as one hollows out a log to make a boat, they hollowed out their minds so that they could receive the teaching. At this point no one spoke. They were silent as they waited for Shakyamuni Buddha to begin his explanation.

H2 The true suchness which is relied upon is the source of the dharma.

Sutra:

The Buddha said, "Ananda, you should know that the wonderful nature is perfect and bright, apart from all names and appearances. Basically there is no world, nor are there any living beings.

Commentary:

The Buddha said, "Ananda, you should know that the wonderful nature is perfect and bright. The Buddha-nature, the self-nature, the bright nature of enlightenment – all refer to this wonderful nature which is **apart from all names and appearances.**" As the *Vajra Sutra* puts it,

> Whatever has an appearance is empty and false. If one sees all appearances as having no appearance, one sees the Thus Come One.

But you can't get rid of appearances. Whatever you see you become attached to. That's why there are appearances. Basically there are no appearances in the wonderful nature. Nor are there any names. Why aren't there any names or appearances? **Basically there is no world, nor are there any living beings.** Only because one gives rise to delusion and creates karma is there a world in which living beings undergo retribution.

Sutra:

"Because of falseness, there is production. Because of production, there is extinction. The names 'production' and 'extinction' are false.

Commentary:

Because of falseness, there is production. Because of production, there is extinction. If there were no production, there would be no extinction. **The names "production" and "extinction" are false.** Production after production, extinction after extinction are all created from falseness; there is no reality to them.

Sutra:

"**When the false is extinguished, there is truth, which is called the Thus Come One's Unsurpassed Bodhi and Great Nirvana: those are names for two kinds of turning around.**

Commentary:

When the false is extinguished, there is truth. When your truth reaches the true suchness of the self-nature, you have reached the Buddha-nature, **which is called the Thus Come One's Unsurpassed Bodhi and Great Nirvana: those are names for two kinds of turning around.** One turns afflictions into bodhi; one turns birth and death into nirvana.

H3 Defiled conditions arise and become the turning wheel.
I1 He exhorts Ananda to recognize two causes for being upside-down.

Sutra:

"**Ananda, you now wish to cultivate true samadhi and arrive directly at the Thus Come One's parinirvana. First, you should recognize the two upside-down causes of living beings and the world. If these upside-down states are not produced, then there is the Thus Come One's true samadhi.**

Commentary:

Ananda, you now wish to cultivate true samadhi and arrive directly at the Thus Come One's parinirvana. You want to cultivate the great bodhisattva's dharma and obtain genuine samadhi power. You want to go right to the Buddha's position and obtain the four virtues of nirvana: permanence, bliss, true self, and purity. **First, you should recognize the two upside-down causes of living beings and the world. If these upside-down states are not produced, then there is the Thus Come One's true samadhi.** To be able to recognize these inversions and to avoid giving rise to them, is the true samadhi of the Buddha.

I2   He clarified the two causes for being upside-down, in detail.
J1   He makes it clear that living beings are upside-down.
K1   From the true they give rise to the false.

Sutra:

"**Ananda, what is meant by the upside-down state of living beings? Ananda, the reason that the nature of the mind is bright is that the nature itself is the perfection of brightness. By adding brightness, another nature arises, and from that false nature, views are produced, so that from absolute nothingness comes ultimate existence.**

Commentary:

Ananda, what is meant by the upside-down state of living beings? Ananda, the reason that the nature of the mind is bright is that the nature itself is the perfection of brightness. The basic nature is perfectly bright and illumines all appearances. But **by adding brightness, another nature arises.** By adding brightness to the inherent brightness of the self nature, another nature comes into being – that of karmic obstructions. This is because from the true the false arises. Based in the nature of the treasury of the Thus Come One, one gives rise to ignorance. Another way of putting it is that one tries to add brightness to enlightenment when all along the nature of enlightenment is brightness itself. In that one movement of the false thought to add light to brightness, the appearance of karma is created, the first of the three subtle appearances.

And from that false nature, views are produced. This is the appearance of turning. Originally there was the nature of the treasury of the Thus Come One, but now ignorance has arisen. Ignorance is a kind of delusion, and once there is delusion, a lack of clarity, then karma arises. The nature of that karma is false, and from it views arise. Birth and death come into being.

> From a single unenlightened thought
> the three subtle appearances arise.

Then external states become the conditions
for the arising of the six coarse appearances.

This concept was also discussed earlier in the sutra. When falseness arises from within the truth, then the appearance of karma is produced. With the appearance of karma, there comes the appearance of turning. First one gives rise to delusion, but then one creates karma and after that must undergo a retribution. So the last is the appearance of manifestation. These are the three subtle appearances:

1. the appearance of karma;
2. the appearance of turning;
3. the appearance of manifestation.

From this process, a great deal of confusion arises, which extends itself into the six coarse appearances:

1. the appearance of knowing, which refers to worldly knowledge;
2. the appearance of continuation, in which things go on and on without cease;
3. the appearance of attaching and grasping;
4. the appearance of reckoning names;
5. the appearance of the arising of karma;
6. the appearance of the suffering of being bound by karma.

So that from absolute nothingness comes ultimate existence. That is the third subtle appearance, that of manifestation. Because of the falseness, existence comes into being.

Sutra:

"All that exists comes from this; every cause in fact has no cause. Subjective reliance on objective appearances is basically groundless. Thus, upon what is fundamentally unreliable, one sets up the world and living beings.

Commentary:

All that exists comes from this. "This" refers to ignorance, because:

From a single unenlightened thought
the three subtle appearances arise.
Then external states become the conditions
for the arising of the six coarse appearances.

"All that exists," then, refers to these appearances. Yet, **every cause in fact has no cause.** "Cause" here refers to a place of reliance. Why is there said to be no cause? It is because, although the three subtle appearances are said to arise from ignorance, ignorance is not really dependable. It is not a true place of reliance. Ignorance itself is a false creation, an empty appearance. Therefore, although it seems to be that the three subtle appearances arise out of ignorance, it doesn't really happen that way, because ignorance itself doesn't even exist! Since ignorance doesn't have any substance of itself, how can the three subtle appearances arise from it? **Subjective reliance on objective appearances is basically groundless.** Living beings are the subjective aspect that relies on ignorance, the objective aspect. But basically there is no foundation in this. There is really no source. **Thus, upon what is fundamentally unreliable, one sets up the world and living beings.** Basically there is nothing to be depended on, but it is on this unreliable ignorance that the world is established. Out of what is empty, false, and unreal the world is set up, and with it all living beings. Their very existence is empty and false; there is nothing real about it.

K2 They confuse their origin so it is difficult to return.

Sutra:

"Confusion about one's basic, perfect understanding results in the arising of falseness. The nature of falseness is devoid of substance; it is not something which can be relied upon.

Commentary:

Confusion about one's basic, perfect understanding results in the arising of falseness. "Confusion" refers to the arising of falseness out of truth. Basically there is no name or appearance in the nature of the treasury of the Thus Come One. But when ignorance is produced, confusion results. Since one is confused, one no longer recognizes one's inherent enlightened nature. Once that happens, it is as if one has lost one's home. Then falseness arises. **The nature of falseness is devoid of substance; it is not something which can be relied upon.** Although falseness arises out of truth, falseness itself doesn't have any substance. It came out of truth, but it is merely illusory. Since ignorance doesn't have a substance of its own, the three subtle appearances cannot really be based on it.

Sutra:

"One may wish to return to the truth, but that wish for the truth is already a falseness. The real nature of true suchness is not a truth that one can seek to return to. By doing so one misses the mark.

Commentary:

One may wish to return to the truth, but that wish for the truth is already a falseness. Basically, ignorance has no substance of its own, and as a consequence the three subtle appearances aren't really based on anything. Therefore, it is a mistake to decide that you want to "return to the truth," to go back to the source in order to seek for the truth. You've just given rise to more falseness. If you want to return to the truth, you should merely refrain from adding brightness to enlightenment; just don't add a head on top of a head. Don't go looking for a donkey while riding on a donkey. **The real nature of true suchness is not a truth that one can seek to return to.** It's not that you decide to return to inherent truth. Rather, you simply dispense with ignorance; that itself is the truth. There's no need to seek further. The entire reason you do not grasp the truth is that you are possessed with ignorance. If you discover that ignorance has no substance, then "you don't get rid of false thinking, and you don't seek the truth." All you have to do is destroy ignorance, and the dharma nature manifests. **By doing so one misses the mark.** Basically one does not have to seek truth or cut off falseness. All one has to do is smash through ignorance, and one's enlightened nature appears spontaneously. But if one does not smash through ignorance and yet seeks the truth, one is doing what is called "letting go of the root and grasping at the branches." The first step is to break through ignorance. When ignorance is destroyed, the three subtle appearances also disappear, and so do the six coarse appearances. How can one seek truth when one has not destroyed ignorance? If one tries to do it that way, one ends up with more false appearances.

K3 They produce karma which brings a retribution.

Sutra:

"**What basically is not produced, what basically does not dwell, what basically is not the mind, and what basically are not phenomena arise through interaction. As they arise more and more strongly, they form the propensity to create karma. Similar karma sets up a mutual stimulus. Because of the karma thus generated, there is mutual production and mutual extinction. That is the reason for the upside-down state of living beings.**

Commentary:

What basically is not produced refers to the ignorance which produces appearances. **What basically does not dwell** refers to karmic consciousness, which is to say the eighth consciousness. **What basically is not the mind** refers to the aspect of seeing. **What basically are not phenomena** refers to the aspect of appearances. Ignorance, karmic consciousness, and the aspects of seeing and appearances have no source and no substance of their own. Their very existence is illusory. Nonetheless, this sickness is contagious once it arises: that is what is meant by they **arise through interaction.** It is the same as the interconnection of the eyes, ears, nose, tongue, body, and mind. **As they arise more and more strongly, they form the propensity to create karma.** Their continual arisal and transformation become powerful, and, so similarly, the karma they make increases. Ignorance, karmic consciousness, and the aspects of seeing and appearances aid one another; they borrow strength from one another. This interaction becomes stronger and stronger until, when it reaches its peak, they become fused and create karma. Karmic obstacles arise. **Similar karma sets up a mutual stimulus. Because of the karma thus generated, there is mutual production and mutual extinction.** Because of this interconnection and mutual stimulation, production and extinction are created. **That is the reason for the upside-down state of living beings.** That's how living beings come to be and how they give rise to inversions.

J2 He makes clear the world is upside-down.
K1 He explains the meaning of the word world.

Sutra:

"**Ananda, what is meant by the upside-down state of the world? All that exists comes from this; the world is set up because of the false arising of sections and shares. Every cause in fact has no cause; everything that is dependent has nothing on which it is dependent, and so it shifts and slides and is unreliable. Because of this, the world of the three periods of time and four directions comes into being. The union and interaction of time and direction bring about changes which result in the twelve categories of living beings.**

Commentary:

Ananda, what is meant by the upside-down state of the world? Ananda, I will explain the inversions of the world. You should listen to this. **All that exists comes from this.** "This" refers to ignorance. "All that exists" refers to the physical bodies and faculties of living beings. **The world is set up because of the false arising of sections and shares** – of ignorance and living beings. "Sections" refers to the individual bodies of living beings. "Shares" refers to their various lifespans. When beings give rise to ignorance, to an unenlightened thought, it is as if they have taken some drug which confuses them, or as if they had gotten drunk on too much wine. They no longer know what they should be doing. So they simply go along with their karma. Whatever karma they create, they undergo retribution for those deeds. This is why the world comes into being. **Every cause in fact has no cause; everything that is dependent has nothing on which it is dependent, and so it shifts and slides and is unreliable.** Although ignorance is groundless and void, nonetheless it is the cause of this world. "No cause," then, refers to ignorance, which, being empty, cannot form a cause. And yet, illusory though it is, it gives rise to the world – "every cause." The world is empty, too, then, and since it is empty, it cannot be relied upon. And yet, it appears it can be relied upon. "Everything that is dependent has nothing on which it is dependent." Basically, the world is not something on which anything can be dependent, but because living beings give rise to false attachment and false emotion, they become something "that is dependent." This dependency is a manifestation of their karmic consciousness. But since the whole situation is basically empty, basically non-existent, basically causeless and unreliable, things "shift and slide and are unreliable." The entire circumstance is never-ending and always in a state of flux. **Because of this, the world of the three periods of time and four directions comes into being.** All these influences combine to create the world. The world has three periods of time: past, present, and future. It also has four aspects of space: the four directions. **The union and interaction of time and direction bring about changes which result in the twelve categories of living beings.** They borrow on one another's strength. The twelve categories of living beings will be discussed below.

K2 He shows its characteristic is constant flux.

Sutra:

"That is why, in this world, movement brings about sounds, sounds bring about forms, forms bring about smells, smells bring about contact, contact brings about tastes, and tastes bring about awareness of mental constructs. The random false thinking resulting from these six creates karma, and this continuous revolving becomes the cause of twelve different categories.

Commentary:

That is why, in this world, movement brings about sounds. Because of the appearance of movement, the defiling object of sounds arises. **Sounds bring about forms.** Once the defiling object of sounds exists, the defiling object of forms comes into being. **Forms bring about smells.** Forms influence the arising of smells. **Smells bring about contact, contact brings about tastes, and tastes bring about awareness of mental constructs. The random false thinking resulting from these six creates karma.** The "six" refer to forms, sounds, smells, tastes, contact, and mental constructs. These six create scattered false thoughts and together they play tricks. They are a gang of thieves. They plunder and rob. They create karma. **And this continuous revolving becomes the cause of twelve different categories.** The interactions of the six defiling organs make continuous karma, which divides into twelve distinct types. From this, beings undergo continual rebirth in the six paths.

Sutra:

"And so, in the world, sounds, smells, tastes, contact, and the like, are each transformed throughout the twelve categories to make one complete cycle.

Commentary:

And so, in the world, sounds, smells, tastes, contact, and the like – that is, forms, sounds, smells, tastes, contacts, and mental constructs – **are each transformed throughout the twelve categories to make one complete cycle.** There is one change after another as they go through the twelve categories, until a complete revolution is made.

These changes can be explained in two ways: first, each defiling sense-object relates to each category of beings, so that there are womb-born sounds, egg-born sounds, and so forth, up to and including womb-born mental constructs, and egg-born mental constructs. The other explanation is that each kind of being complete with the six faculties goes through each category of rebirth in a sequence, based on the weight of its particular karma. Thus if one's thinking is predominant, one becomes first an egg-born being, and so forth.

CHAPTER 5

The Twelve Categories of Living Beings

K3 He explains the retributions of the categories of beings.
L1 He lists the names of the categories of beings.

Sutra:

"The appearance of being upside-down is based on this continuous process. Therefore, in the world there are those born from eggs, those born from wombs, those born from moisture, those born by transformation, those with form, those without form, those with thought, those without thought, those not totally endowed with form, those not totally lacking form, those not totally endowed with thought, and those not totally lacking thought.

Commentary:

The appearance of being upside-down is based on this continuous process. The mutual interaction of the six defiling objects and the twelve categories of living beings brings about the appearance of the upside-down state. **Therefore, in the world there are those born from eggs, those born from wombs, those born from moisture, those born by transformation.** These are four categories of birth.

There are four conditions necessary for birth from an egg to occur:

1. the condition of a father;
2. the condition of a mother;
3. the condition of individual karma;
4. the condition of warmth.

There are three conditions necessary for birth from wombs to occur:

1. the condition of a father;
2. the condition of a mother;
3. the condition of individual karma.

There are two conditions necessary for birth from moisture to occur:

1. the condition of individual karma;
2. the condition of moisture.

Birth by transformation needs only one condition:

1. the condition of individual karma.

Based on one's own karmic consciousness, one transforms as one wishes. One can appear and disappear at will. The next four categories of living beings are **those with form, those without form, those with thought,** and **those without thought,** also **those not totally endowed with form** – it's not that they have form, and yet it's not that they lack form, **those not totally lacking form, those not totally endowed with thought, and those not totally lacking thought** – it's not that they have thought, and yet it's not that they lack thought. These are the twelve categories of living beings. Because time is limited, each category cannot be described in great detail. A simple explanation will have to suffice.

L2	He explains the retributions of the categories of beings.
M1	A specific listing of the categories of beings.
N1	Egg-born.

Sutra:

"Ananda, through a continuous process of falseness, the upside-down state of movement occurs in this world. It unites with energy to become eighty-four thousand kinds of random thoughts that either fly or sink. From this there come into being the egg kalalas which multiply throughout the lands in the form of fish, birds, amphibians, and reptiles, so that their kinds abound.

Commentary:

Ananda, through a continuous process of falseness, the upside-down state of movement occurs in this world. We have learned that falseness arises out of truth, and that out of ignorance arise the three subtle and six coarse appearances, which in turn become numerous empty false appearances. Within the turning cycle of rebirth this process goes on continuously. The arising of karma belongs to movement, so movement is a further creation of the upside-down state. **It unites with energy to become eighty-four thousand kinds of random thoughts that either fly or sink.** "Energy" refers to the karma that is created. "Thoughts that fly" refers to the category of birds and the like. "Thoughts that sink" refers to the category of reptiles and amphibians. **From this** – because of all these scattered thoughts – **there come into being the egg kalalas.** "Kalala" is a Sanskrit word that means "slippery coagulation"; it refers to the foetus resulting from the union of the male semen and female blood in its first week of development. Birth from an egg is a result of thought and the four conditions listed above. These kalalas **multiply throughout the lands in the form of fish, birds, amphibians, and reptiles.** They multiply and spread everywhere. Fish swim in the water, birds fly in the air, and frogs, which can live both in and out of the water, are amphibians. Snakes and turtles belong to the reptile class. These kinds of beings multiply until **their kinds abound**. They spread throughout all the lands of the world.

N2 Womb-born.

Sutra:

"**Through a continuous process of defilement, the upside-down state of desire occurs in this world. It unites with stimulation to become eighty four thousand kinds of random thoughts that are either upright or perverse. From this there come into being the womb arbudas, which multiply throughout the world in the form of humans, animals, dragons, and immortals until their kinds abound.**

Commentary:

This passage discusses womb-born beings. Womb-born beings exist because of emotion. When emotional love reaches its peak and intercourse results, the womb-born being is conceived. Human beings, animals, dragons, and immortals are born in this way. **Through a continuous process of defilement, the upside-down state of desire occurs in this world.** "Defilement" refers to what is unclean, disorderly, and confused. The "continuous process" can refer to the six paths of rebirth, or it can refer to a single being's cycle, a rebirth among humans, animals, dragons, and immortals. Thoughts of love and desire are upside-down. Doing what one should not do is to be upside-down. Doing what is against the law or not in accord with dharma is to be upside-down. The desire **unites with stimulation to become eighty four thousand kinds of random thoughts that are either upright or perverse.** "Stimulation" refers to the creation of karma – to the acting out of the desire. **From this there come into being the womb arbudas, which multiply throughout the world in the form of humans, animals, dragons, and immortals until their kinds abound.** Birth from a womb – that of mammals – is a result of emotion and the three conditions of father, mother, and individual karma. Warmth, a condition necessary for egg-born beings, is not necessary for birth from a womb. "Arbuda" is a Sanskrit word which means "globule" and refers to the foetus in its second week of development. These kinds of beings – humans, animals, dragons, and immortals – spread throughout every land.

N3 Moisture-born.

Sutra:

"Through a continuous process of attachment, the upside-down state of inclination occurs in this world. It unites with warmth to become eighty-four thousand kinds of random thoughts that are vacillating and inverted. From this there come into being through moisture the appearance of peshis, which multiply throughout the lands in the form of insects and crawling invertebrates, until their kinds abound.

Commentary:

This passage discusses beings born from moisture. Birth from moisture is a result of warmth and the two conditions of individual karma and moisture. **Through a continuous process of attachment, the upside-down state of inclination occurs in this world.** "Attachment" refers to clinging and being unable to change. Beings whose natures are attached undergo the turning wheel of rebirth. "Inclination" refers to a tendency to go in certain directions or toward certain things. The inclination **unites with warmth to become eighty-four thousand kinds of random thoughts that are vacillating and inverted.** "Warmth" refers to the creation of karma. "Vacillating" means fluttering. "Inverted" means covered. **From this there come into being through moisture the appearance of peshis, which multiply throughout the lands in the form of insects and crawling invertebrates, until their kinds abound.** "Peshi" is a Sanskrit word which means "soft flesh"; it refers to all initial stage of development of beings born from moisture. "Insects and crawling invertebrates" refer to small worms, bugs, and microscopic-organisms – simple forms of life. These creatures breed in ponds and pools or whereever there is moisture. They are found everywhere throughout the world.

Ordinary people cannot observe it, but all twelve types of beings are in fact interrelated. People have a connection with all these other kinds of beings.

N4 Transformation-born.

Sutra:

"Through a continuous process of change, the upside-down state of borrowing occurs in this world. It unites with contact to become eighty-four thousand kinds of random thoughts of new and old. From this there come into being through transformation the appearance of ghanas, which multiply throughout the lands in the form of metamorphic flying and crawling creatures, until their kinds abound.

Commentary:

This section discusses birth by transformation. Only one condition is required, the condition of individual karma. If one's karma is such that one delights in what is new and grows tired of what is old, then birth by transformation can occur. So it is that some mice can be transformed into bats. Some birds can turn into fish or amphibians. Caterpillars can turn into butterflies. This kind of upside-down state among creatures causes them to change and transform. **Through a continuous process of change, the upside-down state of borrowing occurs in this world.** Because there is a borrowing back and forth, changes and transformations take place among creatures. **It unites with contact to become eighty-four thousand kinds of random thoughts of new and old.** Some creatures despise the old and enjoy the new. They get tired of what is old and want to trade it for something new. And so a bird may tire of being a bird and wish to change into an amphibian, such as a frog. Some caterpillars, grubs, or maggots tire of being worms and want to change into insects, such as butterflies. Some mice tire of being mice and want to change into bats. These are all examples of the birth of beings by transformation. **From this there come into being through transformation the appearance of ghanas, which multiply throughout the lands.** "Ghana" is a Sanskrit word which means "solid flesh," referring in this case to the bodies of metamorphic beings. All the subsequent categories of beings use the term "ghana" to represent their development. These transformation-born beings spread throughout the world **in the form of metamorphic flying and crawling creatures, until their kinds abound.** Crawling creatures turn into flying creatures; flying creatures can turn into creatures that swim. They transform among one another, and their kinds abound.

N5 Having form.

Sutra:

"Through a continuous process of restraint, the upside-down state of obstruction occurs in this world. It unites with attachment to become eighty-four thousand kinds of random thoughts of refinement and brilliance. From this there come into being the ghanas of appearance that possess form, which multiply throughout the lands in the form of auspicious and inauspicious essences, until their kinds abound.

Commentary:

This section discusses beings with form. **Through a continuous process of restraint, the upside-down state of obstruction occurs in this world.** "Restraint" refers to detaining and hindering. Many circumstances unite to form an obstruction. **It unites with attachment to become eighty-four thousand kinds of random thoughts of refinement and brilliance.** "Attachment" refers to the actualizing of karma. These kinds of beings are extremely intelligent. **From this there come into being the ghanas of appearance that possess form, which multiply throughout the lands.** This kind of solid flesh has form. These beings appear **in the form of auspicious and inauspicious essences, until their kinds abound.** These brilliant beings have form, and sometimes it is extremely auspicious for people to see them, though it may be very inauspicious for other people to see them. Although these beings have form, they are not a common sight. Fireflies and pearl-producing oysters are examples of this category of beings. Even though they are rarely seen, they do exist. These kinds of living beings also abound in the universe.

N6 Without form.

Sutra:

"**Through a continuous process of annihilation and dispersion, the upside-down state of delusion occurs in this world. It unites with darkness to become eighty-four thousand kinds of random thoughts of obscurity and hiding. From this there come into being the ghanas of formless beings, which multiply throughout the lands as those that are empty, dispersed, annihilated, and submerged until their kinds abound.**

Commentary:

This section discusses beings without form; it refers to beings in the heavens of the formless realm. **Through a continuous process of annihilation and dispersion, the upside-down state of delusion occurs in this world.** Although "annihilation and dispersion" implies total negation, so that one sees nothing, there still exists, nonetheless, a consciousness and karma, which are what these beings are composed of. Therefore, there is rebirth. "Delusion" refers to a lack of clarity, which comes about because of ignorance and through being upside-down. **It unites with darkness to become eighty-four thousand kinds of random thoughts of obscurity and hiding.** Imperceptibly there is karma which invisibly becomes these myriad random thoughts. "Obscurity and hiding" means that these thoughts are not easy to detect. **From this there come into being the ghanas of formless beings, which multiply throughout the lands.** They spread through every land, **as those that are empty, dispersed, annihilated, and submerged until their kinds abound.** "Empty" refers to beings in the Heaven of Boundless Emptiness. "Dispersed" refers to beings in the Heaven of Boundless Consciousness. "Annihilated" refers to beings in the Heaven of Nothing Whatsoever, and "submerged" refers to beings in the Heaven of Neither Thought Nor Nonthought. So these are beings of the heavens of the four stations of emptiness in the formless realm. These beings are endowed with a karmic consciousness, but no physical form. These beings, too, abound in the world.

N7 Having thought.

Sutra:

"Through a continuous process of illusory imaginings, the upside-down state of shadows occurs in this world. It unites with memory to become eighty-four thousand kinds of random thoughts that are hidden and bound up. From this there come into being the ghanas of those with thought, which multiply throughout the lands in the form of spirits, ghosts, and weird essences, until their kinds abound.

Commentary:

Through a continuous process of illusory imaginings, the upside-down state of shadows occurs in this world. This passage refers to beings born with thought, but without physical form. These are such beings as spirits, ghosts, and weird essences. In the beginning these beings come about because of shadows that **unites with memory to become eighty-four thousand kinds of random thoughts that are hidden and bound up.** They are hidden away, and no one is aware of them. Their random thoughts mass together, and **from this there come into being the ghanas of those with thought, which multiply throughout the lands in the form of spirits, ghosts, and weird essences, until their kinds abound.** "Those with thought" does not refer to the kind of thought necessary for birth from an egg. The kind of thought referred to here is false thinking that is created. Some ghosts and spirits are devious, and some behave properly. Some ghost kings are even manifestations of bodhisattvas, while others are actually unreliable beings. "Weird essences" however, are totally unorthodox and devious. Sometimes people are referred to in this way, indicating that they are not wholesome or good. The manifestation of these weird essences are eerie unpredictable portents. Their kinds are so many one could never describe them all. The retinue of such creatures fills up every corner of the world.

N8 Without thought.

Sutra:

"**Through a continual process of dullness and slowness, the upside-down state of stupidity occurs in this world. It unites with obstinacy to become eighty-four thousand kinds of random thoughts that are dry and attenuated. From this there come into being the ghanas of those without thought, which multiply throughout the lands as their essence and spirit change into earth, wood, metal, or stone, until their kinds abound.**

Commentary:

Through a continual process of dullness and slowness, the upside-down state of stupidity occurs in this world. Obtuseness and dullness create an entire cycle from which arise the *li, mei,* and *wang liang* ghosts. The karma wrought from stupidity **unites with obstinacy to become eighty-four thousand kinds of random thoughts that are dry and attenuated.** They simply dry up mentally. **From this there come into being the ghanas of those without thought, which multiply throughout the lands as their essence and spirit change into earth, wood, metal, or stone, until their kinds abound.** Because their thought is dry and attenuated, their very essence and spirit transform into earth, wood, metal, or stone. These kinds of beings are also found everywhere. How can their essence and spirit turn into these things?

In Hong Kong there's a place called Wang Fu mountain[1]. The story goes that a certain woman's husband enlisted in the navy and never returned to her. But every day she would go stand on this mountain and gaze out to sea. Every day she would stand there gazing and holding her child until eventually her thought became so attenuated that her essence underwent a transformation, and she

---

[1]. The name means "gazing out to watch him return."

turned to stone. To this day you can see the rock shaped like the woman with the child on her back. She's still gazing. It's not at all easy to convince people that one's spirit and essence can turn into earth, wood, metal, or stone, but in fact it can. It really does happen. There are many instances of people turning into stone. There's another way this can happen, too. If, for example, a person has a fiery temper, and the fire of his nature reaches a peak, his very essence can transform into coal. The fire in his nature is so intense that he becomes a substance that is easily burned. People are composed of metal, wood, water, fire, and earth, and if they remain in constant contact with any one element and become too much involved in it, they can turn into that very element. It happens because of attachment and attenuated thoughts. When that phenomenon occurs, can that being ever become a person again? Yes, but one knows not how long it will take. It would involve an extremely long period of time.

N9 Not totally having form.

Sutra:

"Through a continuous process of parasitic interaction, the upside-down state of simulation occurs in this world. It unites with defilement to become eighty-four thousand kinds of random thoughts of according and relying. From this there come into being those not totally endowed with form, who become ghanas of form which multiply throughout the lands until their kinds abound, in such ways as jellyfish that use shrimp for eyes.

Commentary:

This section discusses living beings who are not totally endowed with form. **Through a continuous process of parasitic interaction, the upside-down state of simulation occurs in this world. It unites with defilement to become eighty-four thousand kinds of random thoughts of according and relying.** "According and relying" refers to a mutual dependence. **From this there come into being those not totally endowed with form, who** become ghanas of form which multiply throughout the lands until their kinds abound. They are not totally endowed with form, but through a parasitic interaction they become involved with a being that is endowed with form. These beings appear **in such ways as jellyfish that use shrimp for eyes.** The jellyfish doesn't have any eyes in its physical makeup, so it borrows the eyes of the shrimp, by allowing a parasitic relationship. Jellyfish often look like mere bubbles in the water, but they actually belong to this category of beings: those not totally endowed with form. There are all kinds of beings all over the place that fall into this category.

N10 Not totally without form.

Sutra:

"**Through a continuous process of mutual enticement, an upside-down state of the nature occurs in this world. It unites with mantras to become eighty-four thousand kinds of random thoughts of beckoning and summoning. From this there come into being those not totally lacking form, who take ghanas which are formless and multiply throughout the lands, until their kinds abound, as the hidden beings of mantras and incantations.**

Commentary:

This category is those not totally lacking form. Basically they have no form, except when they are beckoned by mantras. **Through a continuous process of mutual enticement, an upside-down state of the nature occurs in this world.** There is an interaction which is enticing to both. This perversion of the nature results in a union **with mantras to become eighty-four thousand kinds of random thoughts of beckoning and summoning.** Recently I talked about the function of "hooking and summoning," which is another name for what is being discussed here. One beckons by calling the name of the being. Usually one does not see such beings, but when one recites a mantra, the being reveals its form. When they reveal themselves, one can often see them. Although we speak of these creatures as being "ghosts and spirits," they are a special kind of mantra spirit, as we can see from this passage of text. **From this there come into being those not totally lacking form, who take ghanas which are formless and multiply throughout the lands, until their kinds abound.** "Those not totally lacking form" refers to this category of ghosts and spirits – be they dharma protectors or deviant spirits. They are **the hidden beings of mantras and incantations.** In the Secret school there exist mantras which summon these kinds of beings.

N11 Not totally with thought.

Sutra:

"Through a continuous process of false unity, the upside-down state of transgression occurs in this world. It unites with unlike formations to become eighty-four thousand kinds of random thoughts of reciprocal interchange. From this there come into being those not totally endowed with thought, which become ghanas possessing thought and which multiply throughout the lands until their kinds abound in such forms as the varata, which turns a different creature into its own species.

Commentary:

Through a continuous process of false unity, the upside-down state of transgression occurs in this world. It unites with unlike formations to become eighty-four thousand kinds of random thoughts of reciprocal interchange. The two are different, but they change formation to become the same. "Eighty-four thousand" is a general number that is used for each category of being, but in fact each category contains tremendously many kinds of beings – an incalculable number. **From this there come into being those not totally endowed with thought, which become ghanas possessing thought and which multiply throughout the lands until their kinds abound.** To begin with, the creature did not conceive of itself as becoming a certain kind of being, but through a process of thought it becomes a certain type of being. This refers to beings **in such forms as the varata, which turns a different creature into its own species.** "Varata" is a Sanskrit term for a kind of wasp. This wasp takes silk worm caterpillars and transforms them into its own young. It puts the caterpillars in its mud nest and for seven days recites a mantra which says, "Be like me, be like me." At the end of that period, the change takes place. They are called beings not totally endowed with thought, because the caterpillars do not initially think they will turn into wasps. In the *Book of Poetry* (*Shi Jing*) there is the phrase:

> The wasp owes its offspring to the caterpillar.

The wasp steals the caterpillars and removes them to its nest where it uses the mantra to transform them.

N12 Not totally without thought.

Sutra:
"**Through a continuous process of enmity and harm the upside-down state of killing occurs in this world. It unites with monstrosities to become eighty-four thousand kinds of random thoughts of devouring one's father and mother. From this there come into being those not totally lacking thought, who take ghanas with no thought and multiply throughout the lands, until their kinds abound in such forms as the dirt owl, which hatches its young from clods of dirt, and the Pou Jing bird, which incubates a poisonous fruit to create its young. In each case, the young thereupon eat the parents.**

Commentary:
This is the twelfth category of beings – those not totally lacking thought. They have thought, but it is totally warped. Their very spirit is twisted. **Through a continuous process of enmity and harm the upside-down state of killing occurs in this world.** You injure me, and I'll injure you. You kill me, and I'll kill you. You hate me, and I hate you. **It unites with monstrosities to become eighty-four thousand kinds of random thoughts of devouring one's father and mother.** When this hate has built to the point that it permeates everything, then weird creatures come into being. **From this there come into being those not totally lacking**

thought, who take ghanas with no thought and multiply throughout the lands, until their kinds abound. They appear **in such forms as the dirt owl, which hatches its young from clods of dirt.** The owl is known in China as the "cat-headed hawk" and as "the unfilial bird." This bird lays no eggs, but incubates a clod of dirt and is able to bring its young out of it. The problem is that when these young dirt owls hatch, they devour their mother. That's why the bird is called unfilial. **The Pou Jing bird, which incubates a poisonous fruit to create its young.** There is an animal in China called the *pou jing* that looks like a wolf but is smaller. This animal can't reproduce, either, so it takes the fruit from a poisonous tree and can incubate it to create its young. **In each case, the young thereupon eat the parents.** But the case is the same: the young eat the mother. This unfilial beast is perhaps the one being referred to in the text. "Bird" may be a mistranslation. These kinds of beings can be found in every country.

M2 Reiterates their name and number.

Sutra:

"These are the twelve categories of living beings."

Commentary:

Above have been explained **the twelve categories of living beings.**

General Index

A

Accomplishment Buddha 92
Akshobhya Buddha 78, 92
Amitabha Buddha
    as Du Xun 56—57
    as the teaching host 92
Amitabha Sutra 59

B

begging
    gets rid of greed 38—39
bhikshu
    meanings of 139
    see four parajikas
bhikshunis
    are women 17
    see eight parajikas
Bhrukuti 79
billionaires
    are not as good as a Buddha 131
birth
    from eggs 175
    from moisture 175
    from womb 175
Blue Dirgha 79
Bodhisattva
    four vast vows of 72
    Han Shan and Shi De 35—37
    secret practices 54
    should not reveal themselves 35, 57—58
Brahma, lord 79

Buddha
    imposters 12

C

climbing on conditions 8

D

demonic state 86
demons 157—158
    advocate sexual desire 14—15
    mislead others 13—14
deviant
    practices 32—33
Dharma-ending Age 3, 51
Du Xun, Dharma Master 54—57

E

eight difficulties 117
eight great evil stars 148
eight parajikas 139—140
eight sufferings 116
evil stars 146, 148

F

Feng Kan, abbot 35
Five Great Heart Mantras 93, 124
five kinds of pure meat 22—24
five pungent plants 136
five quick causes 162
five rebellious acts 138—139
five slow causes 162

four kinds of birth 174—175
four methods of gathering in 52—54
four parajikas 139
four rules of deportment 64
four vast vows, of a Bodhisattva 72, 81
four virtues of nirvana 164

G

Ganesha 79
ghana 179
ghosts 182
   are predominantly yin 130
giving
   three kinds of 52—53
Great Strength, Bodhisattva
   as Yin Guang 59
Guan Di Gong, dharma-protector 21
Guan Shi Yin, Bodhisattva 79
   as Madam Green 55
   as the fishmonger 6—7
Guo Qing, monastery 35

H

Han Shan 36
Hell of Pulling Out Tongues 62
hundred grains 28

I

icchantika 50
ignorance
   creates the world 170—171
   dispensing with 168—169
incense 75

K

kalala 176
kataputanas, ghosts 129

ku, sorcery 124, 125
kumbhandas, ghosts 130
Kundalin 79

L

living beings
   avoiding products of 26
living beings, categories of
   egg-born 176—177
   womb-born 177—178
   moisture-born 178—179
   transformation-born 179—180
   having form 180—181
   without form 181—182
   having thought 182—183
   without thought 183—184
   not totally having form 184—185
   not totally without form 185—186
   not totally with thought 186—187
   not totally without thought 187—188
Lotus Sutra 6

M

Maitreya, Bodhisattva 78
Matangi 53, 69
meat
   see five kinds of pure meat
milk products 26
mind
   three evils 65
mouth
   four evils 65

N

Nature of Medicine 32
New Buddhism 37

P

Papiyan 18
patience
  with abuse 45
people
  origins of 27—28
peshi 178
Pin Na, dharma protector 79
pishachas, ghosts 130
pou jing, bird 188
Production-of-Jewels Buddha 92
Pu Tou, mountain 59
putanas, ghosts 129

Q

Qie Lan, Bodhisattva 21
Qing, dynasty 58

R

rakshashas, ghosts 129
reciting
  single-mindedly 66
Relentless Hell 41
retribution
  of being blind, mute and deaf 49—50
  of lying 62

S

saving living beings
  see four methods of gathering in
sexual desire
  should be severed 15—17
Shakra, God 79
Shakyamuni Buddha 92
  and the horse-feed retribution 42—43
  and the starving tiger 45
Shi De 36

Shurangama Mantra
  five divisions 92
  five major dharmas 92—94
  responses 142—151
Shurangama Sutra
  demon spotting mirror 29
  six coarse appearances 166
  six defiling objects
    creates karma 172—173
  sorcery 124
spirits 182
  are predominantly yang 130
  causes for 20, 21
spiritual mantra
  and good roots 68

T

tala, tree 50
teachers, deviant 3—4
  and sexual desire 6
thoughts
  should be controlled 8
three subtle appearances 166
three sufferings 51
Tian Tai, mountain 35
transformation 183
twelve categories of living beings
  see living beings, categories of
twenty-eight constellations 147—148

U

Ucchushma 79
Universal Worthy, Bodhisattva
  as Old Mother Pig 56
Uttarakuru 117

V

Vajra Sutra 6, 163

varata 186
vegetarianism 135
Vinayaka 79, 126

W

Wang Fu, mountain 183
Wei Tuo, Bodhisattva 90
Wu Tai, mountain 55, 56

Y

yakshas, ghosts 129
Ye Jia, dharma protector 79
Yin Guang, Dharma Master 58—60

The Shurangama Sutra's Authenticity
by the Venerable Master Hsuan Hua

The Great Master Han Shan (Silly Mountain) once said: "Unless you read the Lotus Sutra, you won't know of the pains the Thus Come One took to save the world. Unless you read the Shurangama Sutra, you won't know the key to cultivating the mind and awakening from confusion." This says it exactly right, because every dharma that exists is found within the Shurangama Sutra, so there are no potentials it fails to attract. It is the essential Dharma for all generations: It is the right seal for becoming a Buddha or a Patriarch. A Chan cultivator must thoroughly master this text and understand the Fifty Skandha-demon States that it explains, in order to escape the snares of the demon-kings. Otherwise, he won't recognize states when they arise, and he will become attached to them and join the retinue of demons. This is extremely dangerous!

We want to be able to recite the Shurangama Mantra from memory, and we also want to memorize the Shurangama Sutra. As the saying goes, "Familiarity leads to expertise." When the time comes, we will gain infinite advantages and inconceivable responses. Anyone who studies Chinese literature simply must read the Shurangama Sutra. The literary quality of this Sutra is excellent, and its meanings are profound; it is the most perfect Sutra.

There are some pretentious scholars who possess no deep understanding of Buddhism and yet consider themselves experts in the field. They see themselves as authorities when they are not. Without a thorough grasp of the principles of Buddhism, they freely criticize the Shurangama Sutra, recklessly asserting that it is an inauthentic Sutra. Still others who may be more conscientious, nonetheless, parrot the false claims of the scholars, like the blind following the blind. The situation is truly pathetic!

Why would anybody claim that the Shurangama Sutra was not spoken by Shakyamum Buddha? It's because the principles explained in this Sutra are simply too true. They thoroughly describe people's problems, thus preventing the goblins, demons, "cow-faced ghosts," and "snake-bodied spirits" from running amok and exposing them for what they are. That's why certain individuals defame the Sutra by claiming that it is fraudulent, destroying people's faith in the Shurangama Sutra so that they themselves have a chance to survive. If they acknowledged that the Sutra was, in fact, spoken by the Buddha, they would have no way to follow its Dharma. First, they cannot uphold the Four Unalterable Aspects of Purity. Second, they cannot cultivate the Dharma-doors of Perfect Penetration of the Twenty-five Sages. Third, they cannot face the Fifty States of the Skandha-demons.

If everyone reads the Shurangama Sutra and understands it, then the spiritual powers of the externalists will lose their magical gleam; they will seem powerless and people will no longer believe that they possess spiritual powers. That's why the celestial demons and externalists have no recourse but to slander the Shurangama Sutra and circulate the spurious claim that it is an unauthentic text.

Not only do laypeople slander the Shurangama Sutra as false, even left-home people perpetuate the rumor. Why? Because most left-home people have received limited education; some are even illiterate and cannot understand the Buddhas' Sutras. This is especially the case with the Shurangama Sutra: its text is deep, its principles are profound, so many cannot understand it or judge its authenticity. Thus, whenever someone claims that a certain Sutra is unauthentic, these ignorant people simply repeat what they hear without giving it any consideration. This is how the Shurangama Sutra has comes to receive its undeserved bad reputation.

In the past, the rulers of India considered the Shurangama Sutra a national treasure and forbade its being carried out of India. Travelers were stopped at the borders and thoroughly searched, out of fear that the Sutra would circulate. Sangha members who were leaving the country were especially subject to the scrutiny of the border guards.

In those days (during the Tang Dynasty in China) the eminent monk, Master Paramiti of India, after racking his brains and thinking up every possible means, finally hid the Sutra beneath the skin of his arm to fool the customs inspectors so that it could come to China. He arrived in Canton, and met a Prime Minister named Fang Rong, who had been exiled by the Empress Wu Zetian and was serving as a Magistrate in Canton. Magistrate Fang Rong requested the Venerable Paramiti to translate the Sutra. He himself acted as editor and turned out a masterpiece of literature, which he then presented in offering to the Empress Wu Zetian. Just at that time, China was experiencing a scandal regarding the Great Cloud Sutra, a fraudulent text. Empress Wu Zetian concealed the translation in the palace and did not allow it to circulate.

Later, when Dhyana Master Shenxiu was appointed as National Master, he sat in the palace to receive offerings. One day he discovered the Sutra, realized its value for meditators in the Chan School, and put it into circulation. Only then did the Shurangama Sutra finally become known in China. The Shurangama Sutra is said to be the last of the Buddha's Sutras to reach China, but during the Dharma-ending Age, it will be the first Sutra to disappear into oblivion. Following it, the other Sutras will gradually disappear as well, until only the Amitabha Sutra will be left.

The Shurangama Mantra
The Efficacious Language of Heaven and Earth

Lectures by the Venerable Master Hsuan Hua
Edited and Translated by the Editorial Committee
of the Buddhist Text Translation Society
In Memory of the First Anniversary of
the Nirvana of Venerable Master Hsuan Hua
and the 20th anniversary of the City of Ten Thousand Buddhas
Burlingame, CA: Buddhist Text Translation Society,
Dharma Realm Buddhist University,
Dharma Realm Buddhist Association, 1996.

Now I am explaining the Shurangama Mantra for you and it is extremely difficult to encounter such a rare Dharma assembly as this. Billions of eons pass and no one explains the Shurangama Mantra even once. Nor is it easy to explain even once. When I am explaining, I know full well that no one understands what's being said. Even if there are those who think they do, they don't really understand. Some think they already understand and so they don't pay attention, but that's also failing to understood.

Among the Buddha's teachings, the Shurangama Mantra is considered to be the king of mantras because it is the longest and most important. The flourish or demise of Buddhism rests entirely with the Shurangama Mantra. It is the efficacious phrases of the Shurangama Mantra that keep heaven and earth from being destroyed. It is the efficacious phrases of the Shurangama Mantra that keep the world from coming to an end. That is why I often tell you that as long as a single person can recite the Shurangama Mantra, the world cannot be destroyed, nor can Buddhism. But when there is no longer anyone who can recite the Shurangama Mantra, then very quickly the world will be destroyed, because the Proper Dharma no longer abides.

Now there are even heavenly demons and externalists who claim that the Shurangama Sutra and the Shurangama Mantra are false. These heaven demons and externalists send their demon sons and grandsons to stir up rumors that cause people to not believe in the Shurangama Sutra and the Shurangama Mantra. This sutra and mantra are critically important to the preservation of the Proper Dharma. The Shurangama Sutra was spoken for the sake of the Shurangama Mantra. There's no way to ever finish expressing the importance of the Shurangama Sutra and the Shurangama Mantra; to the ends of all time their merits, virtues, and wonderful functions could never be told – so absolutely inconceivable and ineffable are they! When all is said and done, the Shurangama Sutra is an ode to the Shurangama Mantra. As long as there is even one person who can recite the Shurangama Mantra, the demons, ghosts, and strange entities don't dare show themselves in this world. They fear the mantra. But when not even one person can recite the Shurangama Mantra by heart, then those weird entities, those demons and ghosts will come out of hiding. Depraved and up to no good, they will not be recognized by most people. At this point in time, since there are still those who can recite the mantra from memory, those malevolent beings haven't made their appearance yet. And so, if you want to keep the world from being destroyed, quickly learn the Shurangama Mantra and read the Shurangama Sutra to keep the Proper Dharma in the world.

Today the explanation of the Shurangama Mantra is beginning. The word "Shurangama" translates as "Ultimately firm and strong."

The entire title of the Shurangama Mantra is "Great White Canopy of Light Dharani Mantra" (*mo he sa dan tuo bo da la tuo lo ni zhou*). It is also called "Brilliant Buddha's Crown, Great White Canopy of Light, Unsurpassed Spiritual Mantra." The

Buddha's Crown refers to the transformation Buddha atop the Buddha's crown. There is no way to conceive the subtle wonder of the mantra. The content of the Shurangama Mantra subdues heavenly demons and controls externalists. Every line, from beginning to end, is the Buddhas' mind-ground Dharma-door. Each line has its own function; each possesses its own esoteric wonder; and each is endowed with incredible power. The recitation of a single word, a single line, a single assembly, or the recitation of the entire mantra causes the heavens to vibrate and the earth to tremble; it's said that heaven and earth are shocked, the ghosts and spirits wail, the demons keep a wide distance, and mountain and river sprites hide away. That brilliance at the Buddha's crown represents the power of the mantra that can dispel every sort of darkness and that enables people to amass all kinds of merit and virtue. If you can accept and uphold the Shurangama Mantra, then you will definitely become a Buddha in the future. You will certainly attain the Unsurpassed Proper and Equal Right Enlightenment. If you continually recite the Shurangama Mantra, then you can get rid of your karmic obstacles from last life and all past lives. That's the incredible function of the Shurangama Mantra!

Mo he is Sanskrit and means "Great." The substance, appearance and function are all great. The substance is said to be great because it pervades the ten directions; the function fills up empty space and reaches throughout the Dharma Realm; and the appearance – well, there isn't any appearance. You can say that it neither has any appearance nor lacks any appearance. The function also doesn't really exist, yet there isn't any place its function doesn't reach in all of space and the Dharma Realm. That's a great function, a great appearance, and a great substance. Pervading the ten directions, exhausting the limits of space, and filling the Dharma Realm is the meaning of "mo he."

Sa dan tuo, also Sanskrit, means "white" and represents purity and lack of defilement. Pure white Dharma is devoid of filth. The Shurangama Mantra is pure white Dharma.

Bo da la is also Sanskrit and translates as "canopy." Canopy is an analogy. This canopy provides shelter for those with myriad virtues. The function of this canopy is to protect those endowed with virtue and those practicing virtuous conduct, meaning anyone who encounters this mantra. Those lacking virtuous conduct won't have an opportunity to meet with this Dharma. It's said:

> *The three lights universally illumine,*
> *permeating the three forces.*
> *In all this world of Jambudvipa*
> *you may not come upon it.*
> *Only those with great virtue*
> *and great goodness will attain it.*
> *Those lacking virtue and goodness*
> *just won't understand it.*

The three lights universally illumine, permeating the three forces. Here, the three lights do not refer to the sun, moon, and stars. Rather, it means that when you recite the Shurangama Mantra, your body emits light, your mouth emits light, and your mind emits light. It is talking about the light of the three karmas. The three forces refer to heaven, earth, and people. *In all this world of Jambudvipa you may not come upon it.* Throughout our world, Jambudvipa, you may seek but not find it. You absolutely must uphold the Shurangama Mantra in order to attain this light. If you have amassed virtuous conduct and have magnanimous virtue, then you will be able to attain the Dharma-door. *Those lacking virtue and goodness just won't understand it.* If you don't have sufficient virtue and haven't done enough good deeds, then even if you come face-to-face with it, you'll miss your chance. Right within arms' reach, you'll lose it. Having come upon gold you'll mistake it for copper; having found a diamond, you'll think it's a piece of glass. You'll fail to recognize it. You'll look upon the Shurangama Mantra as nothing at all out of the ordinary, and as a consequence won't realize it's the gem of gems, the wonder of wonders! You won't have any concept of the Shurangama Mantra's unfathomable merit and virtue.

Besides the three lights emitted when the three karmas of body, mouth, and mind are pure, there is also a swirling red light. Recitation of the Shurangama Mantra generates a swirling red light. It's described this way:

> *A thousand petaled red lotus supports one's body.*
> *As one sits firmly mounted on a black unicorn.*
> *Seeing this, the hordes of monsters*
>   *go far away to hide.*
> *Dharma Master Ji, the Venerable,*
>   *mastered these wonderful sounds.*

A thousand petaled red lotus supports one's body. When you recite the first twenty-nine lines of the Shurangama Mantra a state occurs wherein a red lotus with a thousand petals manifests and emits red light. *As one sits firmly mounted on a black unicorn.* Upon reciting the Mantra, the person chanting finds himself sitting astride a unicorn. *Seeing this, the hordes of monsters go far away to hide.* No matter what kind of weird creature or demon or ghost it might be, they all flee, not daring to face such a magnificent and awesome manifestation. The Venerable Ji is a well-known High Master in Buddhism. His expert use of this passage of the mantra to subdue heavenly demons and control externalists was extremely efficacious. And so the last line says: *Dharma Master Ji, the Venerable, mastered these wonderful sounds.* This passage of the mantra instructs us to "take refuge with all the Buddhas, all the Bodhisattvas, all the Hearers and Condition-Enlightened Ones, and all the gods throughout empty space and the Dharma Realm." It's a passage that protects the Triple Jewel, and so when you recite it the demons flee and the ghosts don't stop running until they're ten miles away. Not just ten miles, they back off until there's no more room to retreat. They don't dare make trouble; they are forced to behave themselves.

That's a general description of what this passage of mantra is about; the details are even more wonderful.

> *Unendingly miraculous and mysterious,*
> *it's extremely hard to fathom.*
> *This vajra secret language*
> *wells forth from your own nature.*
> *Inside the Shurangama Mantra*
> *is marvelous magic!*
> *Then come five eyes and six penetrations*
> *and the Way opens up.*

Unendingly miraculous and mysterious, it's extremely hard to fathom. The Shurangama Mantra is quite esoteric and its changes and transformations are inexplicable; it's not easy to figure out. *This vajra secret language wells forth from your own nature.* The Shurangama Mantra is the secret within the secret. That's the vajras who come to protect the mantra. Your own nature – it is born from your own Buddha nature. *Inside the Shurangama Mantra is marvelous magic!* The Shurangama Mantra is called an efficacious language because of its spell-binding power. That's what "marvelous magic" is referring to. *Then come five eyes and six penetrations and the Way opens up.* If you can continually uphold the Shurangama Mantra – single-mindedly without entertaining other thoughts – then you can attain the Five Eyes and Six Spiritual Penetrations. You will then experience the inconceivable, unfathomable changes and transformations that occur which ordinary people are totally unaware of. And that's the reason why I hope everyone will learn to read the Shurangama Mantra and memorize it. Why is it that the demons, ghosts, and goblins don't dare show themselves when you recite the Shurangama Mantra? It's so powerful that there isn't a place in all of space or the entirety of the Dharma Realm that isn't flooded with auspicious light. Recitation of the Shurangama Mantra patches up the imperfections in the heavens and the earth. One person reciting the

Shurangama Mantra creates power equivalent to one person. A hundred people reciting create power equivalent to a hundred people. And the weird beings here in this world become very well-behaved. So it's better if more people recite.

It's an unsurpassed spiritual mantra. The negating prefix "un-" actually means "lofty to the utmost; brilliant to the extreme." Peerless radiant illumination piercing the heights is the meaning of "un-". And "surpassed"? Well, there's nothing more esteemed, nothing more venerated. "Spiritual" is what is inconceivable and ineffable, what is awe-inspiring, efficacious and unfathomable. The power of mantras brings a response with the Way. When you recite mantras, something happens. "Brilliant Buddha's Crown, Great White Canopy of Light, Unsurpassed Spiritual Mantra." This means that the light at the crown of the Buddha's head is like a great white canopy that comes to shelter and protect all of us who recite the mantra.

No one understands this mantra, nor can they explain line by line and word by word. But if you want to understand it, I can try my best to explain it to you. The Shurangama Mantra can't be explained in a year's time, or three years' time, or even ten years' time. Now I will explain the general intent of this mantra. This mantra is composed of five assemblies which represent the five directions of east, west, south, north, and center. The east is the vajra division with Akshobhya Buddha as the teaching host. The south is the welling up of jewels division with Welling Up of Jewels Buddha as the teaching host. The center is the Buddha division with Shakyamuni Buddha as the teaching host. The west is the lotus division with Amitabha Buddha as the teaching host. The north is the karma division with Accomplishment Buddha as the teaching host. Altogether these five divisions watch over the five demonic armies that abide in this world. Because of these five demons, the Buddhas split up in five directions to repress these demons. Without the Buddhas, these demons would show themselves here in our world. And so, when you recite the Shurangama Mantra, the five demonic armies in the five directions submit and surrender. They behave themselves and don't dare try to oppose the power of the Shurangama Mantra. The five divisions in the mantra are what make it so fine. But you shouldn't be attached. Your becoming attached won't be so fine.

Within the five assemblies of the Shurangama Mantra are more than thirty sections of Dharmas. Before, when I was in Manchuria, the reason I was able to cure people's illnesses was all because of the power of the Shurangama Mantra. But the Shurangama Mantra cannot be used casually. If used, it's not the entire thing that's used, because within it are, in general, more than thirty different Dharmas. If looked at in detail there are over a hundred.

As to these Dharmas, there's the Dharma of Accomplishment. That means by reciting the Shurangama Mantra, whatever method you are practicing will be perfected; whatever thing you want to do will get done. There's also the Dharma of Increasing Benefits. That means, for example, if you don't have enough resolve for the Way in your practice, by reciting the mantra you can increase your wisdom; increase your Bodhi mind; increase the power of your vows; everything will get better. When you recite the mantra, everything you hope increases will surely do so! It will increase for others, too.

The Dharma of Quelling Disasters means that if a calamity is due, reciting the mantra will make it disappear. The disaster will be quelled. Suppose someone is due to drown in the ocean. Reciting the mantra can change the situation so that he doesn't get drowned. Or you're on a boat that's supposed to sink. Recitation of the mantra can keep the boat from sinking. Or the airplane is supposed to crash, but you are reciting the mantra and so it doesn't. Nonetheless, you have to take responsibility for dispelling the calamities in your own mind. What calamities are there in your mind? Well, if you merely rely on the mantra, but inside you are a bundle of false and malevolent thoughts, scattered and impure thoughts, lustful thoughts, then you certainly haven't expelled the calamities in your own mind. In that case, no mantra is going to work. And so if you want to avoid disasters you must first purify your own mind. The purity of your mind is what really dispels calamities. If you are full of greed, hatred, and stupidity, no mantra is going to be efficacious. Our frame of mind is extremely important. We must be kindhearted and filled with goodness, wishing to help others. Our mind should be wholesome.

The Dharma for Hooking and Summoning is for use when you meet up with heavenly demons and externalists and want to catch them. Just as law enforcement officers catch criminals, so too, the Hooking and Summoning Dharma catches weird creatures, demons, and ghosts. They do something here to harm others or do some bad thing that causes people to get sick and then they run away. But you want to catch them and so you recite the mantra, using the Hooking and Summoning Dharma. Well, no matter how far away from you they are, the Dharma-protecting good spirits, or members of the eightfold division, or some of the eighty-four thousand Vajra Treasury Bodhisattvas will immediately snatch them and bring those demonic beings back. Even then, sometimes they won't give in and you have to use all kinds of expedients to teach and transform them. If you use brute force to subdue them, then that's the lowest grade of dharma, it's not a good method. The best methods don't use any sort of power plays to oppress beings. Don't oppress them and don't contend with them. Don't be like an asura – tough and looking for a fight. Even when you clearly have the power to do so, don't use the dharmas to subdue them. You should use virtuous conduct to influence beings and then teach and transform them.

And finally, there is the Dharma of Subduing. Demons have spiritual penetrations and they also have mantras. You recite your mantra and they recite theirs. But when you use the Shurangama Mantra, you break through all their mantras and subdue them. You use the power to quell them and make them behave. I've told you all before that the Shurangama Mantra has within it a few lines of mantra that rends the nets of demons. Why was the mantra from the Brahma Heavens rendered useless? It was because of the Five

The Shurangama Mantra

Great Hearts Mantra. The Five Great Hearts Mantra destroys the mantras underlying the demons' and externalists' spells and incantations. It doesn't matter what mantra they use, when you recite these lines, their spells are smashed and their mantras become ineffectual. If I wanted to market this Dharma, a million dollars wouldn't even touch my asking price! But I can see that you have a bit of sincerity and so I am transmitting it to you absolutely free. To sum it up, no matter what Dharma you cultivate, you must have the unsurpassed resolve for Bodhi; you must have great kindness and compassion; you must practice great giving and great renunciation. You must not use the powers you gain in practicing the Way to oppress any other person or to squelch any demon, monster, goblin, or ghost. Furthermore, the Dharma of Auspiciousness enables things to go your way when you recite the mantra. Good fortune prevails. Now I've given you an explanation of these Dharmas.

I could talk for several years and never finish describing the good points of this mantra. All Buddhas of the ten directions come forth from the Shurangama Mantra. The Shurangama Mantra is the mother of all Buddhas. It was by means of the Shurangama Mantra that all Buddhas perfected Unsurpassed Proper and Pervasive Enlightened Knowledge. The ability of the Buddhas of the ten directions to create response bodies and go throughout the ten directions turning the Dharma wheel to teach and transform living beings; to rub the crowns of those beings and bestow predictions upon them; to rescue beings from their complex sufferings; to enable beings to escape both large disasters and small calamities – their ability to do all that comes from the power of the Shurangama Mantra Heart. If you want to attain the fruition of Arhatship, you absolutely must recite this mantra to keep demonic things from happening. During the Dharma-ending Age if people can memorize the Shurangama Mantra or encourage others to memorize it, well, fire cannot burn such people and water cannot drown them. No matter how potent a poison, it cannot harm them. For those who recite the Shurangama Mantra, poison turns to sweet dew as soon as it enters their mouths. People who recite the Shurangama Mantra will never get born in bad places, even if they want to. Why is that so? It's because the Shurangama Mantra pulls you back and won't allow you to go. Someone who recites the Shurangama Mantra may never have amassed any blessings or virtue, but, simply because he recites the mantra, the Thus Come Ones of the ten directions will bestow their own merit and virtue upon that person. Wouldn't you call that a bargain? That happens based on the recitation of the Mantra alone. If you recite the Shurangama Mantra, you will continually get to be born at a time when a Buddha is in the world and will be able to immerse yourself in cultivation under that Buddha's guidance.

If your mind is terribly scattered so that you can't concentrate and don't have any samadhi-power, but you think about the Shurangama Mantra and recite it with your lips, the Vajra Treasury King Bodhisattvas will very attentively watch for ways to invisibly help you gradually until your confusion has disappeared and you develop samadhi. They will imperceptibly help you open your wisdom and concentrate your mind to the point that you become crystal clear about all the events spanning the previous eighty-four thousand Ganges' sands of eons.

If you can learn the Shurangama Mantra until you have memorized it fluently – so that you become one with the mantra – then you attain the mantra's samadhi and your recitation will be like flowing water, welling up uninterrupted. If you can do that, then at the very least for seven lives to come you will be as wealthy as America's richest oil magnates. And you say, "That's great! I'm going to learn the mantra right away! I wouldn't mind being a magnate of some kind!" Well, if you are that selfish, then don't even bother learning the mantra. Seven lives pass in the blink of an eye anyway. What should those who learn the Shurangama Mantra be hoping for? You should hope for ultimate Buddhahood; hope to attain the Unsurpassed Proper and Equal Right Enlightenment. Don't be so petty! Actually those who are really dedicated in reciting the Shurangama Mantra are transformation bodies of

Buddhas. Not just any transformation bodies, but those atop the Buddha's crown – transformation bodies of that transformation body! And so you see that the wonderful aspects of the Shurangama Mantra are difficult to express, difficult to conceptualize. Wherever someone is seriously reciting the Shurangama Mantra, a great white canopy will be there in the space above him. If your skill in reciting the mantra is high-level and far-reaching, then when you recite, the canopy will extend for thousands of miles, preventing any disasters or difficulties. If you only have a little skill, then the canopy will be right above your own head protecting you. If you have virtue in the Way, if you are a High Sanghan, then when you recite, the entire nation will be benefitted and no calamities will occur. Or if disasters are unavoidable, big ones will turn into little ones, and the little ones won't even happen.

It doesn't matter if it's a nationwide famine, plague, war, or plunder, all those kinds of disasters will be alleviated. Suppose you were to write out the Shurangama spiritual mantra and place it at the main entrances to the city, or in its watchtowers or other lookout places; suppose you could inspire the nation's inhabitants to show interest in the Shurangama Mantra, so that they bow to and revere it and single-mindedly make offerings to it as if they were offering to the Buddhas themselves; suppose you could get every single citizen to wear the mantra on their person or to keep it in their place of residence; well, if you could do that, all disasters would disappear. Whenever the Shurangama Mantra can be found in a place, the gods and dragons are delighted, and so that place will be free from devastating storms; the crops will produce in abundance; and the populace will be peaceful and happy. That is why I say that the merit and virtue of the Shurangama Mantra is inexpressible; it can't be reckoned in the mind; it can't be cognized in our thoughts. That's the wonder of it!

Basically broken precepts cannot be mended. But if you recite the Shurangama Mantra, you can return to purity. But when I say recite, I don't mean you can just do it casually. You have to attain the mantra-recitation samadhi. The recitation of the mantra must flow forth from your mind and the mantra must flow back into your mind. That's called "the mantra is the mind and the mind is the mantra." Your mind and the mantra become united. There isn't any distinction. It reaches the point where you couldn't forget it if you wanted to. That's called even when not reciting, the recitation continues; when reciting there really isn't any recitation. You recite until there aren't any idle thoughts remaining. The only function of the mind is the recitation of the Shurangama Mantra. That's called meshing with the mind. There are no second thoughts. The flow of the mantra's recitation is like water that flows on in uninterrupted waves. At that point, everything expresses the Mahayana – the sounds of the breezes blowing and the water flowing are all the Shurangama Mantra's Heart Mantra. If you can reach that level, then if you have broken precepts, you will be able to return to pure precepts. You will be endowed with the precepts without going through the formal transmission. If you are someone who doesn't want to progress in your practice, who doesn't want to investigate the Buddhadharma, but you recite the Shurangama Mantra for a period of time, quite naturally you will be inspired to be vigorous; those who lack wisdom can open their wisdom. If you are not pure in your cultivation so that you break your vegetarian practices and violate the precepts, but you have not forgotten the Shurangama Mantra, you will be able to quickly return to purity. If you violated precepts before you began upholding the mantra and prior to receiving the precepts, then once you start reciting the mantra you can completely wipe out all those former offenses, no matter how serious they were, including even the Four Parajikas, the Five Rebellious Acts, the Four or Eight Offenses warranting dismissal from the Sangha, which are basically unpardonable. Not even a hair's breadth of an offense will remain. And so I say that the power of the Shurangama Mantra is beyond all conception or description!

Some people who learn how efficacious the Shurangama Mantra is decide to exclusively recite it and ignore all other aspects of cultivation. That's going overboard. In cultivation, no matter what Dharma it is, you have to keep to the Middle Way. Don't do too much and don't fail to do enough. Although the mantra is definitely efficacious, still, you have to develop samadhi. The Shurangama Sutra describes how efficacious this mantra is, but it also explains the method of returning the hearing to listen to your own nature by cultivating perfect penetration of the ear organ. That's also extremely important. While you are reciting the mantra you should be returning your hearing to listen to your own nature. You must reflect within. Didn't I explain earlier how the mantra becomes the mind and the mind becomes the mantra? The mind and the mantra cannot be separated; they are non-dual. When you get there, then you can attain whatever you seek; everything will go the way you want it to; and you will have success in whatever you undertake. When the mind and the mantra merge into one, then you have actually attained the samadhi of Chan meditation and have acquired real samadhi-power. That is something you should know.

Every line of the Shurangama Mantra contains infinite meanings as well as infinite functions. You should realize that the Shurangama Mantra is the most efficacious language in the world – the efficacious within the efficacious, the esoteric within the esoteric! It is an unsurpassed Dharma Treasure – the gem that can save living beings' lives. It embraces all that exists. From the Buddhas of the ten directions to the Avichi Hell, all the four kinds of sages and six sorts of common realms pay homage to the Shurangama Mantra. None of the ten Dharma realms transcends its scope. All categories of ghosts, spirits, Dharma-protecting deities, Hearers, Condition-enlightened Ones, up to the Buddha Vehicle are contained within the Shurangama Mantra. The Shurangama Mantra contains the names of ghost and spirit kings. When the names of those leaders are recited, all the ghosts and spirits in their retinues become very obedient and behave themselves. They don't dare to make trouble. Reciting the Shurangama Mantra every day can cause demonic beings and weird ghosts throughout the world to settle down and stop harming people. The substance and function of the Shurangama Mantra are all-encompassing. It can be said that within the mantra can be found the entirety of Buddhism's teachings and meanings. If you can understand the Shurangama Mantra, then you have understood the essence of Buddhism's esoteric teachings. All the inconceivable wonders and esoteric phenomena in the universe are contained in the Shurangama Mantra. If you master the Shurangama Mantra, then you don't need to study the esoteric school's white teaching, black teaching, yellow teaching, red teaching or any other teaching. This is the ultimate method of samadhi and the most esoteric Dharma. Unfortunately no one really understands this esoteric Dharma; no one even recognizes it. Most people study it but cannot absorb it; they can only recite it but don't know its meanings. Basically it's not necessary to know the meanings of mantras, you need only realize that they are an ineffable efficacious language.

Being able to recite the Shurangama Mantra is a benefit to all beings. Not being able to recite it, you cannot offer that benefit to beings. Quickly learn it, memorize it, investigate and understand it! Then you will be doing what Buddhist disciples should do. The very best is for those who want to recite the Shurangama Mantra to do it for the sake of the entire world; transfer all the merit to the whole world. There isn't anything more important in Buddhism than the Shurangama Mantra. The Shurangama Mantra is a sure sign of the Proper Dharma. The existence of the Shurangama Mantra ensures the existence of the Proper Dharma. When the Shurangama Mantra is gone, the Proper Dharma is gone. Those who cannot recite this mantra are not worthy of being Buddhist disciples. The Shurangama Mantra is nicknamed "six months' stupor" because for most people it takes a half year of diligent recitation to get it memorized. Those of us who can recite the Shurangama Mantra have been planting and nurturing good roots for countless eons. Being able to memorize it perfectly and never forget it is evidence of those good roots. Without good roots, not only will you not be able to recite it, you will never even hear of the existence of the Shurangama Mantra; or if you hear of it you won't understand it and won't be able to recite it. Truly, then, those who can recite it by heart do have great good roots!

The Shurangama Mantra is a Dharma-door difficult to encounter in billions of eons. For every line we learn and understand, we activate one part of its power. But, then, we must actually put it into practice. However it's not that you try to make use of the mantra's vast efficacy and tremendous power. If you use this Dharma but you don't hold the precepts – like most people who aren't clear about anything and casually kill, steal, are lustful, lie, and indulge in intoxicants, and who only recite the Five Great Hearts Mantra when some crisis happens – then you are defiling the Dharma and there is no merit in that. If you insist on trying to control the ghosts and order the Dharma protectors around, then you're just going to be increasing your own karmic offenses. You will bring calamities down upon yourself. Therefore, the first criterion for people who want to cultivate a Dharma is to hold the precepts and place emphasis on developing virtuous conduct. You must not fight, be greedy, seek, be selfish, pursue your own advantages, or lie. If your virtue in the Way is insufficient but you pretend to be a sage who can transmit teachings, or pass yourself off as the leader of a nation, then your behavior is unacceptable. Nowadays everyone is interested in getting the most magic out of mantras, but they are not attentive to their own moral character. And so in fact their recitation will be ineffectual.

Therefore those who study the Shurangama Mantra Dharma must be proper in their behavior, proper in their intent; must not have defiled thoughts, and must not do impure deeds. They should be very attentive to cultivating purity. If on the one hand they cultivate the Shurangama Mantra and on the other hand they don't follow the rules, then they will get themselves into deep trouble. Everyone should pay close attention to this point. If your intent is not proper and your conduct is not proper, then the Vajra Treasury Bodhisattvas will lose their respect for you and won't protect you. The Buddhas and Bodhisattvas are compassionate and would not hurt any living being or harm beings out of anger. But their attendants – the Dharma-protectors, gods, dragons, ghosts, and spirits will become enraged. Those evil ghosts and evil spirits, upon seeing you cultivating the mantra while committing offenses, will bring disaster and harm down upon you; will make you feel very uncomfortable; will cause you to get in grave trouble; or make you have to undergo a series of misfortunes or a series of retributions. This is really no joking matter! Therefore you must eat vegetarian food and purify yourself. Most of all your mind must be pure. Don't have defiled false thoughts. Maintain physical purity and don't practice defiling dharmas. At all times guard your purity. Don't commit even the slightest infractions of the rules.

Reciting the Shurangama Mantra is more valuable than any amount of gold. Reciting the mantra once is equivalent to tons of gold! But your recitation shouldn't be motivated by greed! If you hold the precepts, then you won't be jealous or obstructive; you won't be greedy or angry and your recitation of the mantra will generate pervasive responses and massive benefits. But if your behavior doesn't accord with the rules, the Dharma protecting good spirits will stay far away from you and when something happens to you they won't pay any attention. Therefore, those who recite the Shurangama Mantra shouldn't be cunning or behave in ways that continually create offenses. At all times they should be open and public-spirited; they should strive to benefit others, not themselves; they should cherish the ideals of Bodhisattvas; and cultivate the practices of Bodhisattvas.

The Shurangama Mantra is extremely efficacious, but it is not that easy to master. First of all you cannot be selfish; next you cannot be out to get your own private gains. You have to be magnanimous and devoid of selfish thoughts. You have to be impartial and not prejudiced. You have to be willing to sacrifice yourself for the sake of others. You have to have the resolve to universally save all living beings. If you can embody the above-listed qualities, then you will have swift success. Pay close attention: you must hold the five precepts and practice the ten good deeds. That's the very least you should do.

It won't work to practice this Dharma if you are not following the rules. If you cultivate this Dharma but you don't behave yourself; if you don't guard the precepts or if you are always having defiled thoughts, then not only will there be no response, not only will you have no success, you will in fact bring disaster down upon yourself. And so when you are cultivating the Shurangama Mantra you must be very attentive to maintain purity with your body, your mouth, and your mind. That's the only way you're going to get a response. You cannot say things that cause schisms or make people in the Way-place uneasy. You must pay attention to all aspects of your behavior, whether walking, standing, sitting, or lying down. It's not all right to always be "washing other peoples' clothes" as it were. Take care of yourself. Look into yourself.

The Shurangama Mantra is an efficacious language. Every line has its own particular efficacy. But you don't need to think: Why don't I get any responses from holding the Shurangama Mantra. Don't pay any attention to whether there are responses or not, just keep reciting it. It's like practicing martial arts, every day you have to practice your punches, regardless of what your skill is like. Skill comes through training. It's impossible to have skill without training. By the same principle, you should cultivate your Dharmas every day, no matter what happens, no matter how busy you are. Don't slack off after you've been at it for a while, losing interest in the Shurangama Mantra. It's certainly not the case that you will have some efficacious response as soon as you begin reciting it. Regardless of whether you perceive any response, you should continue reciting it every day. You must deepen your skill day by day. Success doesn't happen overnight. For instance you have to study for ten, twenty, or even thirty years before you gain real scholarship. It's the same with cultivation. You must keep your mind on your recitation of the mantra, continuing your recitation without ever letting it get cut off. It should be just as important as putting on clothes, eating food, and going to sleep; you shouldn't be able to be without it for a single day. It doesn't matter whether there's any response, because by reciting every day you will gradually have a foundation and quite naturally the mantra will function.

If you hope for its wonderful functions and inconceivable power, then you must not keep having false thoughts, always daydreaming and fantasizing. If you cut off your recitation of the mantra, then you will not be able to attain samadhi. You must use your true mind and practice the Shurangama Mantra with sincerity. What's a true mind? It means that for the sake of reciting the Shurangama Mantra you can forget all about time and even space disappears. You don't know if it's day or night; you don't know if you've eaten or not; you don't know if you've slept or not. You forget everything else. Everything disappears and one thought extends for infinite eons, while infinite eons is one thought. That's the kind of spirit you should have – forgetting to eat and sleep for the sake of cultivating the Shurangama Mantra. In that way you certainly can attain the Shurangama Samadhi. If you cannot be that way, then you aren't really cultivating the Shurangama Dharma-door. You should be that way not only in cultivating the Shurangama Mantra, but in the cultivation of any Dharma door – walking without realizing you are walking; sitting with being aware you are sitting; being unaware that you are thirsty or hungry. "Well," you say, "isn't that just turning into a stupid person?" That's right. It's said,

> *When you learn to be a big idiot,*
> *then you start to have some skill;*
> *Studying until you are as if stupid*
> *is the beginning of real insight.*

If you can learn to be as if stupid, then no matter what Dharma door you cultivate you will attain samadhi and gain some realization. It's just because you are unable to be stupid that you cannot properly enter into samadhi and don't get any response from your cultivation.

When you are developing your skill in reciting the Shurangama Mantra, you may dream of yourself bowing to the Buddhas; or in a dream see the Buddhas emitting light; or dream that you see the Buddha come as rub the crown of your head; or dream that the Buddhas speak Dharma for you; or dream that you see the Bodhisattvas, or Condition-enlightened Ones, or Hearers, or Sagely Sanghans or gods and heavenly generals; or in a dream see yourself ascending into space; or dream that you can fly. All of these are good experiences. Or you may be riding a horse or crossing a river and encounter all sorts of auspicious lights; or there may be other extremely rare appearances that manifest. If you do attain responses such as these, then you should be very careful. You should bring forth the resolve for Bodhi; guard the purity of the karma created by your body, mouth, and mind; and increase your efforts and tighten your skill in reciting the mantra. You should not tell others what kinds of responses you've had in order to get others to believe in you or to think highly of you. It's enough for you yourself to know what responses you've had. If you keep advertising your own merits and selling your cultivation out on the streets, then you are wrong. If you act like that, you leave yourself open and the demons will attack. That's like failing to put your jewels in a safebox. If you leave them at the doorway, then someone is certainly going to steal them. Therefore, we must be very careful in our cultivation of the Buddhadharma. Don't let the heavenly demons and externalists have their way with you. But you can report your experiences to your fellow-cultivators if you are not doing it in order to get famous or rich or to make people respect and praise you.

The Shurangama Sutra says, "If you recite and uphold the Shurangama Mantra until you gain skill and can make it function, then eighty-four thousand Vajra Treasury Bodhisattvas and their retinue of followers will always stay near you and protect you, so that everything you hope for will come true." But the demon kings never give up searching for a hole so they can give you more trouble than you can handle.

In the past, Great Master Hongren, the Fifth Patriarch, was cultivating in Hubei at East Mountain. He upheld the precepts strictly and cultivated with unusual intensity. Once when a group of bandits surrounded the city of Hubei, Great Mater Hongren could bear it no longer and decided to try to save the people in that city. He came down the mountain and walked into that city. As soon as the bandits saw Great Master Hongren coming, they were terrified, dropped their armor and weapons, and fled. Why? Because although Great Master Hongren came alone into the city, the bandits saw an army of heavenly generals and heavenly troops clad in golden armour. It was as if the gods themselves had come down to earth – all donning golden armour and carrying jeweled swords and other awesome weapons. That's what caused the bandits to retreat in such haste. And so, without the use of a single knife, spear, or arrow, he routed the bandits. It was because Great Master Hongren recited the Shurangama Mantra that the bandits found him to be so terrifying. You could say that was a manifestation created by the Vajra Treasury Bodhisattvas or you could say it was the awesome virtue of Great Master Hongren that frightened them. That a cultivator was able to frighten the bandits into retreat without the use of a single soldier or weapon is verification of his genuine skill. How else could there have been such a response in the Way?

Shakyamuni Buddha proclaimed the Shurangama Mantra in order to protect of all of us who have brought forth the initial resolve to study the Way; to aid us in attaining samadhi; to help us be at peace in body and mind; and to keep us out of trouble. Therefore we should never forget this Dharma. We should recite and uphold the Shurangama Mantra with single-minded sincerity. By doing so we are helping to perpetuate the Buddhadharma, to keep the Proper Dharma long in the world.

Buddhist Text Translation Society Publication

Buddhist Text Translation Society
International Translation Institute

http://www.bttsonline.org

1777 Murchison Drive,
Burlingame, California 94010-4504 USA
Phone: (650) 692-5912 Fax: (650) 692-5056

When Buddhism first came to China from India, one of the most important tasks required for its establishment was the translation of the Buddhist scriptures from Sanskrit into Chinese. This work involved a great many people, such as the renowned monk National Master Kumarajiva (fifth century), who led an assembly of over 800 people to work on the translation of the Tripitaka (Buddhist canon) for over a decade. Because of the work of individuals such as these, nearly the entire Buddhist Tripitaka of over a thousand texts exists to the present day in Chinese.

Now the banner of the Buddha's teachings is being firmly planted in Western soil, and the same translation work is being done from Chinese into English. Since 1970, the Buddhist Text Translation Society (BTTS) has been making a paramount contribution toward this goal. Aware that the Buddhist Tripitaka is a work of such magnitude that its translation could never be entrusted to a single person, the BTTS, emulating the translation assemblies of ancient times, does not publish a work until it has passed through four committees for primary translation, revision, editing, and certification. The leaders of these committees are Bhikshus (monks) and Bhikshunis (nuns) who have devoted their lives to the study and practice of the Buddha's teachings. For this reason, all of the works of the BTTS put an emphasis on what the principles of the Buddha's teachings mean in terms of actual practice and not simply hypothetical conjecture.

The translations of canonical works by the Buddhist Text Translation Society are accompanied by extensive commentaries by the Venerable Tripitaka Master Hsuan Hua.

BTTS Publications

Buddhist Sutras. Amitabha Sutra, Dharma Flower (Lotus) Sutra, Flower Adornment (Avatamsaka) Sutra, Heart Sutra & Verses without a Stand, Shurangama Sutra, Sixth Patriarch Sutra, Sutra in Forty-two Sections, Sutra of the Past Vows of Earth Store Bodhisattva, Vajra Prajna Paramita (Diamond) Sutra.

Commentarial Literature. Buddha Root Farm, City of 10 000 Buddhas Recitation Handbook, Filiality: The Human Source, Herein Lies the Treasuretrove, Listen to Yourself Think Everything Over, Shastra on the Door to Understanding the Hundred Dharmas, Song of Enlightenment, The Ten Dharma Realms Are Not Beyond a Single Thought, Venerable Master Hua's Talks on Dharma, Venerable Master Hua's Talks on Dharma during the 1993 Trip to Taiwan, Water Mirror Reflecting Heaven.

Biographical. In Memory of the Venerable Master Hsuan Hua, Pictorial Biography of the Venerable Master Hsü Yün, Records of High Sanghans, Records of the Life of the Venerable Master Hsüan Hua, Three Steps One Bow, World Peace Gathering, News from True Cultivators, Open Your Eyes Take a Look at the World, With One Heart Bowing to the City of 10 000 Buddhas.

Children's Books. Cherishing Life, Human Roots: Buddhist Stories for Young Readers, Spider Web, Giant Turtle, Patriarch Bodhidharma.

Musics, Novels and Brochures. Songs for Awakening, Awakening, The Three Cart Patriarch, City of 10 000 Buddhas Color Brochure, Celebrisi's Journey, Lots of Time Left.

The Buddhist Monthly–Vajra Bodhi Sea is a monthly journal of orthodox Buddhism which has been published by the Dharma Realm Buddhist Association, formerly known as the Sino-American Buddhist Association, since 1970. Each issue contains the most recent translations of the Buddhist canon by the Buddhist Text Translation Society. Also included in each issue are a biography of a great Patriarch of Buddhism from the ancient past, sketches of the lives of contemporary monastics and lay-followers around the world, articles on practice, and other material. The journal is bilingual, Chinese and English.

Please visit our web-site at **www.bttsonline.org** for the latest publications and for ordering information.

The Dharma Realm Buddhist Association

Mission

The Dharma Realm Buddhist Association (formerly the Sino-American Buddhist Association) was founded by the Venerable Master Hsuan Hua in the United States of America in 1959. Taking the Dharma Realm as its scope, the Association aims to disseminate the genuine teachings of the Buddha throughout the world. The Association is dedicated to translating the Buddhist canon, propagating the Orthodox Dharma, promoting ethical education, and bringing benefit and happiness to all beings. Its hope is that individuals, families, the society, the nation, and the entire world will, under the transforming influence of the Buddhadharma, gradually reach the state of ultimate truth and goodness.

The Founder

The Venerable Master, whose names were An Tse and To Lun, received the Dharma name Hsuan Hua and the transmission of Dharma from Venerable Master Hsu Yun in the lineage of the Wei Yang Sect. He was born in Manchuria, China, at the beginning of the century. At nineteen, he entered the monastic order and dwelt in a hut by his mother's grave to practice filial piety. He meditated, studied the teachings, ate only one meal a day, and slept sitting up. In 1948 he went to Hong Kong, where he established the Buddhist Lecture Hall and other Way-places. In 1962 he brought the Proper Dharma to the West, lecturing on several dozen Mahayana Sutras in the United States. Over the years, the Master established more than twenty monasteries of Proper Dharma under the auspices of the Dharma Realm Buddhist Association and the City of Ten Thousand Buddhas. He also founded centers for the translation of the Buddhist canon and for education to spread the influence of the Dharma in the East and West. The Master manifested the stillness in the United States in 1995. Through his lifelong, selfless dedication to teaching living beings with wisdom and compassion, he influenced countless people to change their faults and to walk upon the pure, bright path to enlightenment.

Dharma Propagation, Buddhist Text Translation, and Education

The Venerable Master Hua's three great vows after leaving the home-life were (1) to propagate the Dharma, (2) to translate the Buddhist Canon, and (3) to promote education. In order to make these vows a reality, the Venerable Master based himself on the Three Principles and the Six Guidelines. Courageously facing every hardship, he founded monasteries, schools, and centers in the West, drawing in living beings and teaching them on a vast scale. Over the years, he founded the following institutions:

The City of Ten Thousand Buddhas and Its Branches

In propagating the Proper Dharma, the Venerable Master not only trained people but also founded Way-places where the Dharma wheel could turn and living beings could be saved. He wanted to provide cultivators with pure places to practice in accord with the Buddha's regulations. Over the years, he founded many Way-places of Proper Dharma. In the United States and Canada, these include the City of Ten Thousand Buddhas; Gold Mountain Monastery; Gold Sage Monastery; Gold Wheel Monastery; Gold Summit Monastery; Gold Buddha Monastery; Avatamsaka Monastery; Long Beach Monastery; the City of the Dharma Realm; Berkeley Buddhist Monastery; Avatamsaka Hermitage; and Blessings, Prosperity, and Longevity Monastery. In Taiwan, there are the Dharma Realm Buddhist Books Distribution Association, Dharma Realm Monastery, and Amitabha Monastery. In Malaysia, there are the Prajna Guanyin Sagely Monastery (formerly Tze Yun Tung Temple), Deng Bi An Monastery, and Lotus Vihara. In Hong Kong, there are the Buddhist Lecture Hall and Cixing Monastery.

Purchased in 1974, the City of Ten Thousand Buddhas is the hub of the Dharma Realm Buddhist Association. The City is located in Talmage, Mendocino County, California, 110 miles north of San Francisco. Eighty of the 488 acres of land are in active use. The remaining acreage consists of meadows, orchards, and woods. With over seventy large buildings containing over 2,000 rooms, blessed with serenity and fresh, clean air, it is the first large Buddhist monastic community in the United States. It is also an international center for the Proper Dharma.

Although the Venerable Master Hua was the Ninth Patriarch in the Wei Yang Sect of the Chan School, the monasteries he founded emphasize all of the five main practices of Mahayana Buddhism (Chan meditation, Pure Land, esoteric, Vinaya (moral discipline), and doctrinal studies). This accords with the Buddha's words: "The Dharma is level and equal, with no high or low." At the City of Ten Thousand Buddhas, the rules of purity are rigorously observed. Residents of the City strive to regulate their own conduct and to cultivate with vigor. Taking refuge in the Proper Dharma, they lead pure and selfless lives, and attain peace in body and mind. The Sutras are expounded and the Dharma wheel is turned daily. Residents dedicate themselves wholeheartedly to making Buddhism flourish. Monks and nuns in all the monasteries take one meal a day, always wear their precept sash, and follow the Three Principles:

> *Freezing, we do not scheme.*
> *Starving, we do not beg.*
> *Dying of poverty, we ask for nothing.*
> *According with conditions, we do not change.*
> *Not changing, we accord with conditions.*
> *We adhere firmly to our three great principles.*
> *We renounce our lives to do the Buddha's work.*
> *We take the responsibility to mold our own destinies.*
> *We rectify our lives to fulfill the Sanghan's role.*
> *Encountering specific matters,*
> *   we understand the principles.*
> *Understanding the principles,*
> *   we apply them in specific matters.*
> *We carry on the single pulse of*
> *   the Patriarchs' mind-transmission.*

The monasteries also follow the Six Guidelines: not contending, not being greedy, not seeking, not being selfish, not pursuing personal advantage, and not lying.

International Translation Institute

The Venerable Master vowed to translate the Buddhist Canon (Tripitaka) into Western languages so that it would be widely accessible throughout the world. In 1973, he founded the International Translation Institute on Washington Street in San Francisco for the purpose of translating Buddhist scriptures into English and other languages. In 1977, the Institute was merged into Dharma Realm Buddhist University as the Institute for the Translation of Buddhist Texts. In 1991, the Venerable Master purchased a large building in Burlingame (south of San Francisco) and established the International Translation Institute there for the purpose of translating and publishing Buddhist texts. To date, in addition to publishing over one hundred volumes of Buddhist texts in Chinese, the Association has published more than one hundred volumes of English, French, Spanish, Vietnamese, and Japanese translations of Buddhist texts, as well as bilingual (Chinese and English) editions. Audio and video tapes also continue to be produced. The monthly journal Vajra Bodhi Sea, which has been in circulation for nearly thirty years, has been published in bilingual (Chinese and English) format in recent years.

In the past, the difficult and vast mission of translating the Buddhist canon in China was sponsored and supported by the emperors and kings themselves. In our time, the Venerable Master encouraged his disciples to cooperatively shoulder this heavy responsibility, producing books and audio tapes and using the medium of language to turn the wheel of Proper Dharma and do the great work of the Buddha. All those who aspire to devote themselves to this work of sages should uphold the Eight Guidelines of the International Translation Institute:

1. One must free oneself from the motives of personal fame and profit.
2. One must cultivate a respectful and sincere attitude free from arrogance and conceit.
3. One must refrain from aggrandizing one's work and denigrating that of others.
4. One must not establish oneself as the standard of correctness and suppress the work of others with one's fault-finding.
5. One must take the Buddha-mind as one's own mind.
6. One must use the wisdom of Dharma-Selecting Vision to determine true principles.
7. One must request Virtuous Elders of the ten directions to certify one's translations.
8. One must endeavor to propagate the teachings by printing Sutras, Shastra texts, and Vinaya texts when the translations are certified as being correct.

These are the Venerable Master's vows, and participants in the work of translation should strive to realize them.

Instilling Goodness Elementary School, Developing Virtue Secondary School, Dharma Realm Buddhist University

"Education is the best national defense." The Venerable Master Hua saw clearly that in order to save the world, it is essential to promote good education. If we want to save the world, we have to bring about a complete change in people's minds and guide them to cast out unwholesomeness and to pursue goodness. To this end the Master founded Instilling Goodness Elementary School in 1974, and Developing Virtue Secondary School and Dharma Realm Buddhist University in 1976.

In an education embodying the spirit of Buddhism, the elementary school teaches students to be filial to parents, the secondary school teaches students to be good citizens, and the university teaches such virtues as humaneness and righteousness. Instilling Goodness Elementary School and Developing Virtue Secondary School combine the best of contemporary and traditional methods and of Western and Eastern cultures. They emphasize moral virtue and spiritual development, and aim to guide students to become good and capable citizens who will benefit humankind. The schools offer a bilingual (Chinese/English) program where boys and girls study separately. In addition to standard academic courses, the curriculum includes ethics, meditation, Buddhist studies, and so on, giving students a foundation in virtue and guiding them to understand themselves and explore the truths of the universe. Branches of the schools (Sunday schools) have been established at branch monasteries with the aim of propagating filial piety and ethical education.

Dharma Realm Buddhist University, whose curriculum focuses on the Proper Dharma, does not merely transmit academic knowledge. It emphasizes a foundation in virtue, which expands into the study of how to help all living beings discover their inherent nature. Thus, Dharma Realm Buddhist University advocates a spirit of shared inquiry and free exchange of ideas, encouraging students to study various canonical texts and use different experiences and learning styles to tap their inherent wisdom and fathom the meanings of those texts. Students are encouraged to practice the principles they have understood and apply the Buddhadharma in their lives, thereby nurturing their wisdom and virtue. The University aims to produce outstanding individuals of high moral character who will be able to bring benefit to all sentient beings.

Sangha and Laity Training Programs

In the Dharma-ending Age, in both Eastern and Western societies there are very few monasteries that actually practice the Buddha's regulations and strictly uphold the precepts. Teachers with genuine wisdom and understanding, capable of guiding those who aspire to pursue careers in Buddhism, are very rare. The Venerable Master founded the Sangha and Laity Training Programs in 1982 with the goals of raising the caliber of the Sangha, perpetuating the Proper Dharma, providing professional training for Buddhists around the world on both practical and theoretical levels, and transmitting the wisdom of the Buddha.

The Sangha Training Program gives monastics a solid foundation in Buddhist studies and practice, training them in the practical affairs of Buddhism and Sangha management. After graduation, students will be able to assume various responsibilities related to Buddhism in monasteries, institutions, and other settings. The program emphasizes a thorough knowledge of Buddhism, understanding of the scriptures, earnest cultivation, strict observance of precepts, and the development of a virtuous character, so that students will be able to propagate the Proper Dharma and perpetuate the Buddha's wisdom. The Laity Training Program offers courses to help laypeople develop correct views, study and practice the teachings, and understand monastic regulations and ceremonies, so that they will be able to contribute their abilities in Buddhist organizations.

Let Us Go Forward Together

In this Dharma-ending Age when the world is becoming increasingly dangerous and evil, the Dharma Realm Buddhist Association, in consonance with its guiding principles, opens the doors of its monasteries and centers to those of all religions and nationalities. Anyone who is devoted to humaneness, righteousness, virtue, and the pursuit of truth, and who wishes to understand him or herself and help humankind, is welcome to come study and practice with us. May we together bring benefit and happiness to all living beings.

Dharma Realm Buddhist Association Branches

The City of Ten Thousand Buddhas
P.O. Box 217, Talmage, CA 95481-0217 USA
Tel: (707) 462-0939   Fax: (707) 462-0949
Home Page: http://www.drba.org

Institute for World Religions (Berkeley Buddhist Monastery)
2304 McKinley Avenue, Berkeley, CA 94703 USA
Tel: (510) 848-3440

Dharma Realm Buddhist Books Distribution Society
11th Floor, 85 Chung-hsiao E. Road, Sec. 6, Taipei, Taiwan R.O.C.
Tel: (02) 2786-3022   Fax: (02) 2786-2674

The City of the Dharma Realm
1029 West Capitol Avenue, West Sacramento, CA 95691 USA
Tel: (916) 374-8268

Gold Mountain Monastery
800 Sacramento Street, San Francisco, CA 94108 USA
Tel: (415) 421-6117   Fax: (415) 788-6001

Gold Wheel Monastery
235 North Avenue 58, Los Angeles, CA 90042 USA
Tel: (323) 258-6668

Gold Buddha Monastery
248 East 11th Avenue, Vancouver, B.C. V5T 2C3 Canada
Tel: (604) 709-0248   Fax: (604) 684-3754

Gold Summit Monastery
233 1st Avenue, West Seattle, WA 98119 USA
Tel: (206) 284-6690   Fax: (206) 284-6918

Gold Sage Monastery
11455 Clayton Road, San Jose, CA 95127 USA
Tel: (408) 923-7243   Fax: (408) 923-1064

The International Translation Institute
1777 Murchison Drive, Burlingame, CA 94010-4504 USA
Tel: (650) 692-5912   Fax: (650) 692-5056

Long Beach Monastery
3361 East Ocean Boulevard, Long Beach, CA 90803 USA
Tel: (562) 438-8902

Blessings, Prosperity, & Longevity Monastery
4140 Long Beach Boulevard, Long Beach, CA 90807 USA
Tel: (562) 595-4966

Avatamsaka Hermitage
11721 Beall Mountain Road, Potomac, MD 20854-1128 USA
Tel: (301) 299-3693

Avatamsaka Monastery
1009 4th Avenue, S.W. Calgary, AB T2P OK8 Canada
Tel: (403) 234-0644

Kun Yam Thong Temple
161, Jalan Ampang, 50450 Kuala Lumpur, Malaysia
Tel: (03) 2164-8055 Fax: (03) 2163-7118

Prajna Guanyin Sagely Monastery (formerly Tze Yun Tung)
Batu 5½, Jalan Sungai Besi,
Salak Selatan, 57100 Kuala Lumpur, Malaysia
Tel: (03) 7982-6560 Fax: (03) 7980-1272

Lotus Vihara
136, Jalan Sekolah, 45600 Batang Berjuntai,
Selangor Darul Ehsan, Malaysia
Tel: (03) 3271-9439

Buddhist Lecture Hall
31 Wong Nei Chong Road, Top Floor, Happy Valley, Hong Kong, China
Tel: (02) 2572-7644

Dharma Realm Sagely Monastery
20, Tong-hsi Shan-chuang, Hsing-lung Village, Liu-kuei
Kaohsiung County, Taiwan, R.O.C.
Tel: (07) 689-3717 Fax: (07) 689-3870

Amitabha Monastery
7, Su-chien-hui, Chih-nan Village, Shou-feng,
Hualien County, Taiwan, R.O.C.
Tel: (07) 865-1956 Fax: (07) 865-3426

Verse of Transference

May the merit and virtue accrued from this work,
Adorn the Buddhas' Pure Lands,
Repaying four kinds of kindness above,
And aiding those suffering in the paths below.

May those who see and hear of this,
All bring forth the resolve for Bodhi,
And when this retribution body is over,
Be born together in the Land of Ultimate Bliss.

Dharma Protector Wei Tuo Bodhisattva